Selections from the

BLACK

Book Four

Provocative Selections by Black Writers

College Reading Skills

JAMESTOWN PUBLISHERS

a division of NTC/CONTEMPORARY PUBLISHING GROUP
Lincolnwood, Illinois USA

Books in the *Selections from the Black* Series

Book One   Book Three
Book Two   **Book Four**

ON THE COVER

The art on the cover is an untitled mixed media work on paper by Michele Stutts.

Michele Stutts was born in Liverpool, England in 1959. In 1970 she and her sister immigrated to America with their parents. She recalls the transition as a true culture shock. Her awareness of all the differences was heightened and caused her to express her perceptions of everything around her through her art.

A highly talented artist, Stutts's works have been exhibited and reviewed extensively throughout the Midwest. A 1997 issue of the *International Review of African American Art* listed Stutts as one of the most promising emerging African American artists today.

Acknowledgments, which are on the facing page, are considered an extension of this copyright page.

ISBN: 0-89061-842-9
Published by Jamestown Publishers,
a division of NTC/Contemporary Publishing Group, Inc.,
4255 West Touhy Avenue,
Lincolnwood (Chicago), Illinois 60646-1975, U.S.A.

ACKNOWLEDGMENTS

Acknowledgment is gratefully made to the following publishers, authors, and agents for permission to reprint these works. Every effort has been made to determine copyright owners. In the case of any omissions, the Publisher will be pleased to make suitable acknowledgments in future editions.

"Brothers and Sisters." Excerpt from *In Search of Our Mother's Gardens: Womanist Prose* by Alice Walker. Copyright © 1975 by Alice Walker. Reprinted by permission of Harcourt Brace & Company.

"The Autobiography of Malcolm X." Excerpt from *The Autobiography of Malcolm X* by Malcolm X with Alex Haley. Copyright © 1964 by Alex Haley and Malcolm X. © 1965 by Alex Haley and Betty Shabazz. Reprinted by Random House, Inc.

"Philosophy and Opinions." Excerpt from *Philosophy and Opinions* by Marcus Garvey. (1916)

"I love those little booths at Benevenuti's." From *Blacks* by Gwendolyn Brooks, published by Third World Press, Chicago, 1991.

"Why I Ran Away." Excerpt by Bloke Modisane from *An African Treasury,* edited by Langston Hughes. Copyright © 1960 by Langston Hughes. Published by Crown Publishers, Inc.

"Atlanta Compromise Speech." Excerpt from *Atlanta Compromise Speech* by Booker T. Washington. (1895)

"Dusk of Dawn." Excerpt from Dusk of Dawn by W. E. B. DuBois. Copyright © 1940 by Harcourt, Brace & World. Copyright © 1968 by Shirley Graham DuBois. Reprinted by permission of David G. DuBois.

"Sweet Lorraine." Excerpt from *Sweet Lorraine* by James Baldwin from the introduction to *To Be Young, Gifted and Black* by Lorraine Hansberry. Copyright © 1969 by Prentice-Hall, Inc.

"The Hottest Water in Chicago." Excerpt from *The Hottest Water in Chicago* by Gayle Pemberton. Copyright © 1992 by Gayle Pemberton. Published by Faber and Faber. Reprinted by permission of Gayle Pemberton.

"Women, Race, and Class." Excerpt from *Women, Race, and Class* by Angela Y. Davis. Copyright © 1981 by Angela Y. Davis. Reprinted by permission of Random House, Inc.

"A Touch of Innocence." Text excerpt from *A Touch of Innocence*, copyright © 1959 and renewed 1987 by Katherine Dunham, reprinted by permission of Harcourt Brace & Company.

"Fatheralong." Excerpt from *Fatheralong* by John Edgar Wideman. Copyright © 1994 by John Edgar Wideman.

Reprinted by permission of Pantheon Books, a division of Random House, Inc.

"The Glory Trumpeter." Poem from *The Glory Trumpeter* by Derek Walcott from Collected Poems, 1948-84 by Derek Walcott. Copyright © 1986 by Derek Walcott. Reprinted by permission of Farrar, Straus & Giroux, Inc.

"Showing My Color." Excerpt from *Showing My Color* by Clarence Page. Copyright © 1996 by Clarence Page. Copyright © 1996 by Clarence Page. Reprinted by permission of HarperCollins Publishing, Inc.

"The Origin and Growth of Afro-American Literature, I, II." Excerpts from "The Origin and Growth of Afro-American Literature, I, II" by John Henrik Clarke, *Negro Digest,* December 1967. Copyright © 1967 by John Henrik Clarke. Published by Johnson Publishing Company, Inc. Reprinted by permission of John Henrik Clarke.

"A Century of Negro Portraiture in American Literature." Excerpt from *A Century of Negro Portraiture in American Literature* by Sterling A. Brown. Reprinted from *The Massachusetts Review.* Copyright © 1966 by The Massachusetts Review, Inc.

"Lynch Law in All Its Phases." Excerpts from speech, *Lynch Law in All Its Phases* by Ida B. Wells-Barnett. (1893)

"Indictment of South Africa." Excerpt by Nelson Mandela from *The Political Awakening of Africa.* Copyright © 1964 by Nelson Mandela. Originally appeared in December 22, 1962 issue of *Globe* Magazine.

Author Photographs

Alice Walker: F. Capri/Saga/Archive Photos; Malcolm X: Archive Photos; Marcus Garvey: Archive Photos; Gwendolyn Brooks: Popperfoto/Archive Photos; Booker T. Washington: Archive Photos; W. E. B. DuBois: Archive Photos; James Baldwin: Jack Manning/New York Times/Archive Photos; Angela Y. Davis: Chris Felver/Archive Photos; Katherine Dunham: David Lees/Archive Photos; John Edgar Wideman: University of Wyoming; Derek Walcott: Reuters/Evan Richmand/Archive Photos; Clarence Page: Ernie Cox, Jr.; Sterling A. Brown: Moorland-Spingarn Research Center, Howard University; Ida B. Wells-Barnett: Archive Photos; Nelson Mandela: Reuters/Patrick De Noirmont/Archive Photos.

CONTENTS

1 Introductory Selection

EXPLAINS HOW THE TEXT IS ORGANIZED AND HOW TO USE IT TO MAXIMUM ADVANTAGE

VOCABULARY, PART ONE—

All of these terms are in the selection you are about to read. Study each term and its meaning. Then answer the questions below.

As you read the story, notice how each term is used. You will have more questions about the terms later.

intent, purpose

moderate, calm; avoiding extremes

intervening, coming between

oppression, persecution; great hardship

servitude, a lack of freedom; slavery

efficient, able to perform a task easily and skillfully

consecutively, coming one after another in order

corresponding, matching

diagnostic, helping to analyze or find problems

discriminating, able to see differences and distinctions

1. If you counted from 1 to 100 in order, how would you be presenting the numbers?

   _____

2. Which term would you use if you were talking about the years between, for example, 1968 and 1991? _____

3. Which term could describe a person who works without wasting any effort?

   _____

4. Which term would describe a person who could easily tell the difference between real and fake emeralds? _____

5. Which term could describe a person who takes a middle-of-the-road position on various issues? _____

A READING PURPOSE —

The following passage will tell you something about the selections in this book and how each chapter is structured. As you read, decide which chapter part will be most helpful to you to improve your reading.

(Before you begin reading this selection, turn to page 4 and record the hours and minutes in the box labeled Starting Time at the bottom of the second column. If you are using this text in class and your instructor has made provisions for timing, you need not stop now; read on.)

■

You are using this text for two purposes: (1) to improve your reading and study skills and (2) to read what black people are saying now and what they have said in the past.

Over 20 years ago, when *Selections from the Black* was first published, our nation was just beginning to realize that blacks had a voice and had something to say. The publisher's <u>intent</u> was to assemble selections from black writers and publish them so that our texts might racially balance the other literature that college students were expected to read. When these texts were first published, there were objections from those who felt that a menu of exclusively black writings only served to further isolate African American students from the American mainstream.

Fortunately, <u>moderate</u> thought prevailed, and the concept of a black reading and study skills program was accepted. In the <u>intervening</u> years tens of thousands of students, black and white, have used *Selections from the Black* with satisfaction and success.

In the selections in this series you will read the words of slaves describing their days of <u>oppression</u>. You will read the words of yesterday's leaders—DuBois, Garvey, Washington, and others—and begin to understand the history and background of Negro <u>servitude</u>. You will understand how the thinking of these writers influenced their times and ours.

You will read the words of authors from the more recent past describing the explosive racial climate of the 1950s and 1960s. This text presents the voices of protest, moderate and defiant, including those silenced by death, exile, and imprisonment. Writers of both extremes are presented here because their words have structured and defined black America.

You will also read selections representing the black experience in the 1980s and 1990s, and from these you will get some idea of the way their authors feel life has—and has not—changed. The works of African and Caribbean writers are included as well, including some that deal with South Africa's longstanding white-minority rule and policy of apartheid. These messages from South Africa are important to us because apartheid was long an issue of international proportions and forms a significant part of the total black experience.

> It is important to understand the situation of the black person over time and throughout history.

Black men and women writing about politics, sports, business, journalism, and entertainment have contributed to this series. Also included are many master writers of fiction; their stories, rich with feeling, are part of the treasury of black literature.

In this level of the program you will also find poetry by some of the great black poets. The two poems that are included in this book should be read in much the same way you read fiction selections—that is, sentence by sentence (rather than line by line) and idea by idea. Writers' thoughts are usually expressed more tightly in poetry than in fiction, but by learning the vocabulary and rereading the lines as necessary, you will find you can understand what is being said.

We want you to enjoy these selections, and we want you to learn from them. We especially want you to understand the situation of the black person over time and throughout history.

The other purpose for using this text, that of reading and study improvement, recognizes reality too: the reality of today. This text will help you to develop skills and techniques necessary for efficiency in our society.

Included with each selection is a Study Skills exercise. In these exercises you will learn methods of understanding, critical thinking skills, techniques of comprehension, and many other key ways to improve your reading ability. The Study Skills exercises are designed to assist you in developing efficient reading techniques. As you read the selections in this book, you will find that often one Study Skills exercise leads directly to the next. It is important to read and work the Study Skills exercises consecutively in order to understand fully each subject.

Today's reader must be flexible enough to choose from a supply of skills one that is suitable for each reading task. The skilled reader has learned that each kind of reading matter demands a corresponding reading technique—there is no single "best" way to read. As you complete the selections and exercises in this book, you will find your reading skills growing.

USING THE TEXT

The 20 selections are designed to be read in numerical order, starting with the Introductory Selection and ending with Selection 20. Because the selections increase in difficulty as you progress through the book, the earlier ones prepare you to handle the upcoming ones successfully.

Here are the procedures to follow for reading each selection.

1. Read the Author Notes.

At the beginning of each chapter is a brief biography of the selection's author. This biography will make you familiar with the time and place in which the author was writing as well as his or her special accomplishments and concerns. Reading the biography will help you get more out of the selection.

2. Answer the Vocabulary Questions.

Immediately preceding each selection is a vocabulary previewing activity. The activity includes 10 vocabulary words from the selection, their meanings as they are used in the selection, and 5 questions related to those words. To answer each question, you will choose from and write one of the 10 vocabulary words. Previewing the vocabulary in such a fashion will give you a head start on understanding the words when you encounter them in the selection. The words are underlined for easy reference.

3. Preview Before Reading.

Previewing acquaints you with the overall content and structure of the selection before you actually read. It is like consulting a road map before taking a trip: planning the route gives you more confidence as you proceed and, perhaps, helps you avoid any unnecessary delays. Previewing should take about a minute or two and is done in this way:

a) Read the title. Learn the writer's subject and, possibly, his or her point of view on it.

b) Read the opening and closing paragraphs. These contain the introductory and concluding remarks. Important information is frequently presented in these key paragraphs.

c) Skim through. Try to discover the author's approach to the subject. Does he or she use many examples? Is the writer's purpose to convince you about certain ideas? What else can you learn now to help you when you read?

4. Establish a Reading Purpose.

After you have previewed the selection, establish a purpose for reading the selection. Use the suggestion that precedes the selection; it will help you complete some of the later activities.

5. Read the Selection.

Do not try to race through. Read well and carefully enough so that you can answer the comprehension questions that follow.

Keep track of your reading time by noting when you start and finish. A table on page 122 converts your reading time to a words-per-minute rate. Select the time from the table that is closest to your reading time. Record those figures in the boxes at the end of the selection. Be aware that there is no one ideal reading speed for everything. The efficient reader varies reading speed as the selection requires.

Many of the selections have been reprinted from full-length books and novels. If you find a particular selection interesting, you may enjoy reading the entire book. Complete information is contained in a bibliography on page 121.

6. Answer the Comprehension Questions.

After you have read the selection, find the comprehension questions that follow. These have been included to test your understanding of what you have read. The questions are <u>diagnostic</u> too. Because the comprehension skill being measured is identified, you can detect your areas of weakness.

Read each question carefully and, without looking back, select one of the four choices given that answers that question most accurately or most completely. Frequently all four choices, or options, given for a question are *correct*, but one is the *best* answer. For this reason some comprehension questions are highly challenging and require you to be highly <u>discriminating</u>. You may, from time to time, disagree with an answer. When this happens, you have an opportunity to sharpen your powers of discrimination. Study the question again and seek to discover why the listed answer may be best. When you disagree with the text, you are thinking; when you objectively analyze and recognize your errors, you are learning.

A profitable habit for you to acquire is the practice of analyzing the questions you have answered incorrectly. If time permits, return to the selection to find and underline the passages containing the correct answers. This process helps you to see what you missed the first time. Some interpretive and generalization-type questions are not answered specifically in the text. In these cases bracket the parts of the selections that refer to the correct answers. Your instructor may recommend that you complete this step outside of class as homework.

7. Answer Additional Vocabulary Questions.

Following the comprehension section are two sets of sentences using the 10 vocabulary words introduced earlier. Each fill-in-the-blank sentence requires you to choose the correct word after looking at the context (surrounding words). This format gives you an opportunity to improve your ability to use context as an aid in understanding words. The efficient use of context is a valuable vocabulary tool.

The boxes following the vocabulary activity contain space for your comprehension scores and your scores from this second vocabulary activity. Each correct vocabulary item is worth 10 points, and each correct comprehension answer is worth 10 points.

Pages 123 and 124 contain graphs to be used for plotting your scores and tallying your incorrect responses. On page 123 record your comprehension score at the appropriate intersection of lines, using an X. Use a circle or some other mark on the same graph to record your vocabulary results. Some students prefer to use different color inks or pencil and ink to distinguish between comprehension and vocabulary plottings.

On page 124 darken the squares to indicate the comprehension questions you have missed. By referring to the Skills Profile as you progress through the text, you and your instructor will be able to tell which questions give you the most trouble. As soon as you detect a specific weakness in comprehension, consult with your instructor to see what supplementary materials he or she can provide or suggest.

8. Write About the Selection.

A brief writing activity allows you to offer your own opinions about some aspect of the selection. Here you are always asked to write a few clearly written paragraphs, containing as many specific facts or examples as possible, to complete each writing assignment.

9. Complete the Study Skills Exercises.

Concluding each chapter is a passage on study skills, followed by five completion questions to be answered after you have finished the passage. One or two of these questions will always ask you to apply the study skill to the selection you have just read.

If class time is at a premium, your instructor may prefer that you complete some or all of these activities out of class.

All of the selections in this text are structured just like this introductory one. After completing this selection and its exercises, you will be prepared to proceed to Selection 2.

Starting Time	
Reading Time	
Finishing Time	
■ Reading Rate	

COMPREHENSION —

Read the following questions and statements. For each one, put an X in the box before the option that contains the most complete or accurate answer.

1. How much time should you devote to previewing a selection?
   - [ ] a. Your time will vary with each selection.
   - [ ] b. You should devote about one or two minutes to previewing.
   - [ ] c. No specific time is suggested.
   - [ ] d. None—the instructor times the selection.

2. The way the vocabulary exercises are described suggests that
   - [ ] a. the meaning of a word often depends on how it is used.
   - [ ] b. the final authority for word meaning is the dictionary.
   - [ ] c. words have precise and permanent meanings.
   - [ ] d. certain words are always difficult to understand.

3. The writer of this passage presents the facts in order of
   - [ ] a. importance.
   - [ ] b. purpose.
   - [ ] c. time.
   - [ ] d. occurrence.

4. *Selections from the Black* is based on which of the following premises?
   - [ ] a. Literature for college students needs to be racially balanced.
   - [ ] b. Black students learn best from black writers.
   - [ ] c. The writings of black authors should provoke student interest.
   - [ ] d. Traditional reading improvement texts are racially unfair.

5. How does the writer feel about reading speed?
   - [ ] a. It is a minimal aspect of the total reading situation.
   - [ ] b. It is second (following comprehension) in the ranking of skills.
   - [ ] c. It will vary from selection to selection.
   - [ ] d. It should be developed at an early age.

6. The introductory selection
   - [ ] a. eliminates the need for oral instruction.
   - [ ] b. explains the proper use of the text in detail.
   - [ ] c. permits the student to learn by doing.
   - [ ] d. allows for variety and interest.

7. The introductory selection suggests that
   - [ ] a. most readers are not flexible.
   - [ ] b. students should learn to use different reading skills for different types of reading matter.
   - [ ] c. students today read better than students of the past did.
   - [ ] d. 20 selections is an ideal number for a reading improvement text.

8. The overall tone of this passage is
   - [ ] a. serious.
   - [ ] b. suspenseful.
   - [ ] c. humorous.
   - [ ] d. sarcastic.

9. The author of this selection is probably
   - [ ] a. a doctor.
   - [ ] b. an accountant.
   - [ ] c. an educator.
   - [ ] d. a businessman.

10. The writer of this passage makes his point clear by
- ☐ a. telling a story.
- ☐ b. listing historical facts.
- ☐ c. using metaphors.
- ☐ d. giving directions.

Comprehension Skills
1. recalling specific facts
2. retaining concepts
3. organizing facts
4. understanding the main idea
5. drawing a conclusion
6. making a judgment
7. making an inference
8. recognizing tone
9. understanding characters
10. appreciating literary forms

VOCABULARY, PART TWO—
Write the term that makes the most sense in each sentence.

oppression   intervening

efficient   intent

consecutively

1. The purpose of this book was never to isolate black writers; instead, its _____ was to make them a part of the total curriculum.

2. The _____ years between the first publication of this book and the present have shown that the author's idea was correct.

3. Many of the writers represented in this book suffered _____ .

4. Because the study skills are presented in order, it is important to study each chapter _____ .

5. By applying the study skills as you go, you will become a more _____ reader.

moderate   diagnostic

discriminating   corresponding

servitude

6. Besides slavery, the writers in this book had to endure other types of _____.

7. Responses of the writers to discrimination ranged from _____ to extreme.

8. Mark the box _____ to the right response for each comprehension question.

9. You must be especially _____ between possible answers for some questions.

10. You can use your wrong answers in a _____ way to figure out your reading weaknesses.

Comprehension Score [ ]

Vocabulary Score [ ]

WRITING—
Think about the weaknesses you might have as a reader. In what ways do you think the chapters in this book will be most helpful in overcoming them? Write a few paragraphs explaining what you think. Be as specific as you can.

STUDY SKILLS—
Read the following passage and answer the questions that follow it.

Dictionary Skills
1. Locating Words in Alphabetical Order. One way to speed up word location is to gain proficiency in locating words in alphabetical order. Dictionaries, as you know, list words alphabetically, so the faster you can find a word, the sooner you have the information you need.

2. Using Guide Words. To help you find words quickly, dictionaries print guide words at the top of each page. These tell you the first entry and the last entry for that page. Because entries are listed alphabetically, a glance at the guide words can quickly help you know what words are on that page.

3. Identifying Variant Spellings. Some words can be correctly spelled in more than one way. For example, *traveled* can also be spelled *travelled*. Variant spellings used in England, such as *colour*, are labeled *Brit*. Some dictionaries may only list the more popular form of a word.

4. Choosing the Appropriate Meaning. Most common words have several meanings. One dictionary shows forty-four definitions for the word *go*. You have to choose exactly the right meaning that fits the sense of the material you are reading.

With just a little practice, you will be amazed to find that the simple act of using a dictionary regularly will make your school work easier and markedly improve your grades.

It is important to have a good hard-cover, college-level desk dictionary as a basic reference. Paperback or pocket-sized dictionaries and supermarket giveaways are just not complete enough for use while studying. If you are about to purchase your first dictionary, ask your in-structor for a list of those most frequently recommended for school use.

1. Guide words indicate the first and last word entries on a _____.

2. If only one spelling of a word is offered, it may be the more _____ form.

3. It is important to choose the meaning of the word that is _____ for the material you are reading.

4. For example, for a word like *study,* which this final section of each chapter deals with, you may find as many as ten different _____.

5. It is a good idea to obtain the dictionary that is _____ by your school.

2 | Brothers and Sisters

Alice Walker

AUTHOR NOTES—
Although best known for *The Color Purple,* and other novels, Alice Walker has also written volumes of short stories, poems, and essays. Themes of racism, classism, and sexism are predominant in Walker's work, and her central characters are generally African American women.

Walker received the Pulitzer Prize and the American Book Award in 1983 for *The Color Purple,* which was made into a movie in 1985. She received the Guggenheim Award in 1977, was nominated for the National Book Critics Circle Award in 1982, and has received various writing fellowships. She has also written *In Search of Our Mothers' Gardens: Womanist Prose,* an influential collection of essays that introduced the term *womanism.* Her most recent essay collection is *Anything We Love Can Be Saved* (1997).

VOCABULARY, PART ONE—
All of these terms are in the story you are about to read. Study each term and its meaning. Then answer the questions below.

As you read the story, notice how each vocabulary term is used. You will have more questions about the terms later.

aimless, without purpose

negate, to make nothing of

vacant, showing a lack of intelligence

humiliation, a lowering of one's dignity or self-respect

cleavage, the area between a woman's breasts as revealed by a low neckline

moon, to behave in a dreamy or distracted way

ideology, system of beliefs of a political movement or group

detract, take away from; lessen the value of

dominator, person who has control over others

hypocrite, person who pretends to be good but really isn't

1. Which word describes the walk of someone who roams around without seeming to know where she is going? _____

2. Which word tells what you might suffer if people in your class made fun of a serious proposal you presented? _____

3. Which word names a person who speaks out against violence and then goes home and beats his wife? _____

4. Which word names a person who sets up the laws in a group and then demands that everyone obey them? _____

5. If you break all the windows in a neighbor's building, which word tells what you have done to that building's value? _____

A READING PURPOSE —

In this selection Alice Walker talks about her early family life and her father's influence on his children. As you read, decide whether you agree with the values he tried to pass on to the family.

---

1 We lived on a farm in the South in the fifties, and my brothers, the four of them I knew (the fifth had left home when I was three years old), were allowed to watch animals being mated. This was not unusual; nor was it considered unusual that my older sister and I were frowned upon if we even asked, innocently, what was going on. One of my brothers explained the mating one day, using words my father had given him: "The bull is getting a little something on his stick," he said. And he laughed. "What stick?" I wanted to know. "Where did he get it? How did he pick it up? Where did he put it?" All my brothers laughed.

2 I believe my mother's theory about raising a large family of five boys and three girls was that the father should teach the boys and the mother teach the girls the facts, as one says, of life. So my father went around talking about bulls getting something on their sticks and she went around saying girls did not need to know about such things. They were "womanish" (a very bad way to be in those days) if they asked.

3 The thing was, watching the matings filled my brothers with an <u>aimless</u> sort of lust, as dangerous as it was unintentional. They knew enough to know that cows, months after mating, produced calves, but they were not bright enough to make the same connection between women and their offspring.

■ 4 Sometimes, when I think of my childhood, it seems to me a particularly hard one. But in reality, everything awful that happened to me didn't seem to happen to *me* at all, but to my older sister. Through some incredible power to <u>negate</u> my presence around people I did not like, which produced invisibility (as well as an ability to appear mentally <u>vacant</u> when I was nothing of the kind), I was spared the <u>humiliation</u> she was subjected to, though at the same time, I felt every bit of it. It was as if she suffered for my benefit, and I vowed early in my life that none of the things that made existence so miserable for her would happen to me.

5 The fact that she was not allowed at official matings did not mean she never saw any. While my brothers followed my father to the mating pens on the other side of the road near the barn, she stationed herself near the pigpen, or followed our many dogs until they were in a mating mood, or, failing to witness something there, she watched the chickens. On a farm it is impossible *not* to be conscious of sex, to wonder about it, to dream...but to whom was she to speak of her feelings? Not to my father, who thought all young women perverse. Not to my mother, who pretended all her children grew out of stumps she magically found in the forest. Not to me, who never found anything wrong with this lie.

6 When my sister menstruated she wore a thick packet of clean rags between her legs. It stuck out in front like a penis. The boys laughed at her

> When a double standard is a way of life, it may take part of a lifetime to overcome its effects.

as she served them at the table. Not knowing any better, and because our parents did not dream of actually *discussing* what was going on, she would giggle nervously at herself. I hated her for giggling, and it was at those times I would think of her as dim-witted. She never complained, but she began to have strange fainting fits whenever she had her period. Her head felt as if it were splitting, she said, and everything she ate came up again. And her cramps were so severe she could not stand. She was forced to spend several days of each month in bed.

7 My father expected all of his sons to have sex with women. "Like bulls," he said, "a man *needs* to get a little something on his stick." And so, on Saturday nights, into town they went, chasing the girls. My sister was rarely allowed into town alone, and if the dress she wore fit too snugly at the waist, or if her cleavage dipped too far below her collarbone, she was made to stay home.

8 "But why can't I go too," she would cry, her face screwed up with the effort not to wail.

9 "They're boys, your brothers, *that's* why they can go."

10 Naturally, when she got the chance, she responded eagerly to boys. But when this was discovered she was whipped and locked up in her room.

11 I would go in to visit her.

12 "Straight Pine," she would say, "you don't know what it *feels* like to want to be loved by a man."

13 "And if this is what you get for feeling like it I never will," I said, with—I hoped—the right combination of sympathy and disgust.

14 "Men smell so good," she would whisper ecstatically. "And when they look into your eyes, you just melt."

15 Since they were so hard to catch, naturally she thought almost any of them terrific.

16 "Oh, that Alfred!" she would moon over some mediocre, square-headed boy, "he's so *sweet!*" And she would take his ugly picture out of her bosom and kiss it.

17 My father was always warning her not to come home if she ever found herself pregnant. My mother constantly reminded her that abortion was a sin. Later,

although she never became pregnant, her period would not come for months at a time. The painful symptoms, however, never varied or ceased. She fell for the first man who loved her enough to beat her for looking at someone else, and when I was still in high school, she married him.

18 My fifth brother, the one I never knew, was said to be different from the rest. He had not liked matings. He would not watch them. He thought the cows should be given a choice. My father had disliked him because he was soft. My mother took up for him. "Jason is just tender-hearted," she would say in a way that made me know he was her favorite; "he takes after me." It was true that my mother cried about almost anything.

19 Who was this oldest brother? I wondered.

20 "Well," said my mother, "he was someone who always loved you. Of course he was a great big boy when you were born and out working on his own. He worked on a road gang building roads. Every morning before he left he would come in the room where you were and pick you up and give you the biggest kisses. He used to look at you and just smile. It's a pity you don't remember him."

21 I agreed.

22 At my father's funeral I finally "met" my oldest brother. He is tall and black with thick gray hair above a young-looking face. I watched my sister cry over my father until she blacked out from grief. I saw my brothers sobbing, reminding each other of what a great father he had been. My oldest brother and I did not shed a tear between us. When I left my father's grave he came up and introduced himself. "You don't ever have to walk alone," he said, and put his arms around me.

23 One out of five ain't *too* bad, I thought, snuggling up.

24 But I didn't discover until recently his true uniqueness: He is the only one of my brothers who assumes responsibility for all his children. The other four all fathered children during those Saturday-night chases of twenty years ago. Children—my nieces and nephews whom I will probably never know—they neither acknowledge as their own, provide for, or even see.

25 It was not until I became a student of women's liberation ideology that I could understand and forgive my father. I needed an ideology that would define his behavior in context. The black movement had given me an ideology that helped explain his colorism (he *did* fall in love with my mother partly because she was so light; he never denied it).

Feminism helped explain his sexism. I was relieved to know his sexist behavior was not something uniquely his own, but, rather, an imitation of the behavior of the society around us.

26 All partisan movements add to the fullness of our understanding of society as a whole. They never detract; or, in any case, one must not allow them to do so. Experience adds to experience. "The more things the better," as O'Connor and Welty both have said, speaking, one of marriage, the other of Catholicism.

27 I desperately needed my father and brothers to give me male models I could respect, because white men (for example; being particularly handy in this sort of comparison)—whether in films or in person—offered man as dominator, as killer, and always as hypocrite. ∎

28 My father failed because he copied the hypocrisy. And my brothers—except for one—never understood they must represent half the world to me, as I must represent the other half to them.*

*Since this essay was written, my brothers have offered their names, acknowledgment, and some support to all their children.

Starting Time	
Reading Time	
Finishing Time	
Reading Rate	

COMPREHENSION —

Read the following questions and statements. For each one, put an X in the box before the option that contains the most complete or accurate answer.

1. The author finally met her older brother at a
   □ a. funeral.
   □ b. wedding.
   □ c. party.
   □ d. convention.

2. The writer's father may be classified as
   □ a. hard-working and money-saving.
   □ b. ingenious.
   □ c. having different standards for his sons and daughters.
   □ d. irrational.

3. The writer of this selection organizes details according to
   □ a. simple listing.
   □ b. chronological order.
   □ c. order of importance.
   □ d. cause and effect.

4. Which one of the following would make a good title for the selection?
   □ a. A Great Need
   □ b. Theories of Racism
   □ c. Fallacies of Sex
   □ d. The Failure of a Family

5. How many children were there in the author's family?
   □ a. four
   □ b. five
   □ c. six
   □ d. seven

6. The author's father expected his sons to be
   □ a. sexually promiscuous.
   □ b. socially respected.
   □ c. completely independent.
   □ d. totally refined.

7. This selection implies that, as a youngster, the author was much like her
   □ a. mother.
   □ b. father.
   □ c. sisters.
   □ d. four brothers.

8. The questions asked by the author in the first paragraph suggest an atmosphere of
   □ a. confusion.
   □ b. innocence.
   □ c. jealousy.
   □ d. tragedy.

9. Jason's character may be described as
   ☐ a. flighty.
   ☐ b. humorous.
   ☐ c. responsible.
   ☐ d. aggressive.
10. "My mother took up for him," is another way of saying that Walker's mother
    ☐ a. disliked Jason.
    ☐ b. forgave Jason.
    ☐ c. defended Jason.
    ☐ d. respected Jason.

Comprehension Skills

1. recalling specific facts
2. retaining concepts
3. organizing facts
4. understanding the main idea
5. drawing a conclusion
6. making a judgment
7. making an inference
8. recognizing tone
9. understanding characters
10. appreciating literary forms

VOCABULARY, PART TWO—

Write the term that makes the most sense in each sentence.

vacant	**humiliation**
ideology	**detract**
dominator	

1. Walker's father was a _____ who tried to control every aspect of his daughters' lives.

2. Her sister suffered a lot of _____ because the father would make fun of her.

3. Walker would not let her father's criticism _____ from her feelings of self-worth.

4. Because she could pretend not to understand what was going on around her, as a child Walker could convince people that she was rather _____ .

5. As an adult, she would study the _____ of women's liberation as a way of gaining a stronger system of beliefs and attitudes about herself.

aimless	**cleavage**
moon	**negate**
hypocrite	

6. Because their father had tried to _____ her feelings of self-worth, Walker's sister tried to build herself up in other ways.

7. She would wander around in a(n) _____ manner, waiting for something to fill her time.

8. Often she would wear low-cut dresses that displayed her _____ .

9. She would _____ after every man she met, dreaming about how wonderful they all were.

10. At least she was not a _____ ; she never pretended to be something she wasn't.

Comprehension Score [ ]

Vocabulary Score [ ]

WRITING—

If Alice and Jason had written to each other when Alice was a teenager, what would they have said? Assume that you are either Alice or Jason. Write a short letter telling the other person your feelings about the family. Use specific information from the story in your letter.

STUDY SKILLS—

Read the following passage and answer the questions that follow it.

Editing Your Work, I

After writing a theme or essay, the next step is to read and edit it. This is the time to polish your writing, smooth out the rough spots, and correct any errors.

It is a mistake to suppose that a satisfactory piece of work can result from just one writing. Everyone needs to work from a rough draft, polishing and editing to arrive at a truly finished product. Skilled writers revise several times because they have learned that with each revision, an improved version is produced. At least one rewrite is essential to make a paper acceptable. When proofing and editing the first copy, follow these steps.

1. Read for Effect. After writing your paper, read it aloud to see if your words create the effect intended. Does it sound the way you want it to?

Certain errors of agreement and usage will be obvious when heard out loud. Generally, though, listen for impact, and determine if the paper puts across your ideas in the way you intended.

Review Sentence Structure. Be alert for incomplete thoughts (sentence fragments) and run-on sentences or comma splices. Each sentence should express a complete thought. Excessively long, involved, or unclear sentences confuse the reader. Search for a more concise and accurate way to express your ideas. Look for ways to combine thoughts; connect sentences that are related.

1. After you finish _____ an essay, it needs to be edited.

2. At least one rewrite is _____ to make a paper acceptable.

3. Read the paper aloud to see if it _____ the way you want it to.

4. Look for concise and accurate ways to express your _____ .

5. For instance, in the sentence "He is tall and black with thick gray hair above a young-looking face," Alice Walker presents a clear description of her _____ .

3

The Autobiography of Malcolm X

Malcolm X with Alex Haley

VOCABULARY, PART ONE—

All of these terms are in the story you are about to read. Study each term and its meaning. Then answer the questions below.

As you read the story, notice how each vocabulary term is used. You will have more questions about the terms later.

AUTHOR NOTES—

Malcolm X was born Malcolm Little in 1925. At 21, he was imprisoned for burglary. In prison, he adopted the beliefs of the Black Muslims, a religious group that advocated separation of the races. Following his release, he rose through the ranks of the Black Muslims, but broke with them in 1964 because of disagreements with their leader, the prophet Elijah Muhammad. After a trip to Mecca and conversion to orthodox Islam, Malcolm X organized his own Islamic religious center, the Muslim Mosque, Inc. and changed his name to El-Hajj Malik al-Shabazz. He also formed the Organization of Afro-American Unity, which sought political rights for black Americans. In 1965, he was assassinated at a meeting in Harlem.

The Autobiography of Malcolm X was published in 1965. In 1992, the African American filmmaker Spike Lee released his movie, *X*, which spurred new interest in Malcolm X.

solidarity, a sharing of common interests and goals

instill, give to; teach

incentive, something that motivates people on a course of action

agnostics, people who are not sure whether God exists

hovering, continuing to wait around nearby

subtly, indirectly, without being noticed

conjunction, connection; combination

smugness, self-righteousness

arrogance, excessive display of pride and self-importance

complacency, self-satisfaction without seeing a need for change

1. Which word could name the extra money your employer promised you if you could line up two more people to work for him? _____

2. Which word tells how you would be acting if you helped someone in a quiet, behind-the-scenes way?_____

3. Which word tells what a parent would be doing if she stood over her child as he worked a puzzle, waiting to help if he made a mistake?

   _____

4. Which word defines the attitude of a person who says, "We've always been successful doing things this way; why change now?" _____

5. Which word could be an antonym for *believers?* _____

A READING PURPOSE—

In talking about his vision for the future in this selection, Malcolm X also tells how his ideas have changed over time. As you read, look for some contrasts between his past and present ideas.

---

1 I kept having all kinds of troubles trying to develop the kind of Black Nationalist organization I wanted to build for the American Negro. Why Black Nationalism? Well, in the competitive American society, how can there ever be any white-black <u>solidarity</u> before there is first some black solidarity? If you will remember, in my childhood I had been exposed to the Black Nationalist teachings of Marcus Garvey—which, in fact, I had been told had led to my father's murder. Even when I was a follower of Elijah Muhammad, I had been strongly aware of how the Black Nationalist political, economic and social philosophies had the ability to <u>instill</u> within black men the racial dignity, the <u>incentive</u>, and the confidence that the black race needs today to get up off its knees, and to get on its feet, and get rid of its scars, and to take a stand for itself.

2 One of the major troubles that I was having in building the organization that I wanted—an all-black organization whose ultimate objective was to help create a society in which there could exist honest white-black brotherhood—was that my earlier public image, my old so-called "Black Muslim" image, kept blocking me. I was trying to gradually reshape that image. I was trying to turn a corner, into a new regard by the public, especially Negroes; I was no less angry than I had been, but at the same time the true brotherhood I had seen in the

■ Holy World had influenced me to recognize that anger can blind human vision.

3 Every free moment I could find, I did a lot of talking to key people whom I knew around Harlem, and I made a lot of speeches, saying: "True Islam taught me that it takes *all* of the religious, political, economic, psychological, and racial ingredients, or characteristics, to make the Human Family and the Human Society complete.

4 "Since I learned the *truth* in Mecca, my dearest friends have come to include *all* kinds—some Christians, Jews, Buddhists, Hindus, <u>agnostics</u>, and even atheists! I have friends who are called Capitalists, Socialists, and Communists! Some of my friends are moderates, conservatives, extremists—some are even Uncle Toms! My friends today are black, brown, red, yellow, and *white!*"

5 I said to Harlem street audiences that only when mankind would submit to the One God who created all—only then would mankind even approach the "peace" of which so much *talk* could be heard...but toward which so little *action* was seen.

6 I said that on the American racial level, we had to approach the black man's struggle against the white man's racism as a human problem, that we had to forget hypocritical politics and propaganda. I said that both races, as human beings, had the obligation, the responsibility, of helping to correct

America's human problem. The well-meaning white people, I said, had to combat, actively and directly, the racism in other white people. And the black people had to build within themselves much greater awareness that along with equal rights there had to be the bearing of equal responsibilities.

7 I knew, better than most Negroes, how many white people truly wanted to see American racial problems solved. I knew that many whites were as frustrated as Negroes. I'll bet I got fifty letters some days from white people. The white people in meeting audiences would throng around me, asking me, after I had addressed them somewhere, "What *can* a sincere white person do?"

8 When I say that here now, it makes me think about that little co-ed I told you about, the one who flew from her New England college down to New York and came up to me in the Nation of Islam's restaurant in Harlem, and I told her that there was "nothing" she could do. I regret that I told her that. I wish that now I knew her name, or where I could telephone her, or write to her, and tell her what I tell white people now when they present themselves as being sincere, and ask me, one way or another, the same thing that she asked.

9 The first thing I tell them is that at least where my own particular Black Nationalist organization, the Organization of Afro-American Unity, is concerned, they can't *join* us. I have these very deep feelings that white people who want to join black organizations are really just taking the escapist way to salve their consciences. By visibly hovering near us, they are "proving" that they are "with us." But the hard truth is this *isn't* helping to solve America's racist problem. The Negroes aren't the racists. Where the really sincere white people have got to do their "proving" of themselves is not among the black *victims*, but out on the battle lines of where America's racism really *is*—and that's in their own home communities; America's racism is among their own fellow whites. That's where the sincere whites who really mean to accomplish something have got to work.

10 Aside from that, I mean nothing against any sincere whites when I say that as members of black organizations, generally whites' very presence subtly renders the black organization automatically less effective. Even the best white members will slow down the Negroes' discovery of what they need to do, and particularly of what they can do—for themselves, working by themselves, among their own kind, in their own communities.

> The man who once spoke of "white devils" talks of his vision for the future: whites and blacks solving America's race problem together.

11 I sure don't want to hurt anybody's feelings, but in fact I'll even go so far as to say that I never really trust the kind of white people who are always so anxious to hang around Negroes, or to hang around in Negro communities. I don't trust the kind of whites who love having Negroes always hanging around them. I don't know—this feeling may be a throwback to the years when I was hustling in Harlem and all of those red-faced, drunk whites in the afterhours clubs were always grabbing hold of some Negroes and talking about "I just want you to know you're just as good as I am—" And then they got back in their taxicabs and black limousines and went back downtown to the places where they lived and worked, where no blacks except servants had better get caught. But, anyway, I know that every time that whites join a black organization, you watch, pretty soon the blacks will be leaning on the whites to support it, and before you know it a black may be up front with a title, but the whites, because of their money, are the real controllers.

12 I tell sincere white people, "Work in conjunction with us—each of us working among our own kind." Let sincere white individuals find all other white people they can who feel as they do—and let them form their own all-white groups, to work trying to convert other white people who are thinking and acting so racist. Let sincere whites go and teach non-violence to white people!

13 We will completely respect our white co-workers. They will deserve every credit. We will give them every credit. We will meanwhile be working among our own kind, in our own black communities—showing and teaching black men in ways that only other black men can—that the black man has got to help himself. Working separately, the sincere white people and sincere black people actually will be working together.

14 In our mutual sincerity we might be able to show a road to the salvation of America's very soul. It can only be salvaged if human rights and dignity, in full, are extended to black men. Only such real, meaningful actions as those which are sincerely motivated from a deep sense of humanism and moral responsibility can get at the basic causes that pro-

duce the racial explosions in America today. Otherwise, the racial explosions are only going to grow worse. Certainly nothing is ever going to be solved by throwing upon me and other so-called black "extremists" and "demagogues" the blame for the racism that is in America.

15   Sometimes, I have dared to dream to myself that one day, history may even say that my voice—which disturbed the white man's <u>smugness</u>, and his <u>arrogance</u>, and his <u>complacency</u>—that my voice helped to save America from a grave, possibly even a fatal catastrophe.

16   The goal has always been the same, with the approaches to it as different as mine and Dr. Martin Luther King's non-violent marching, that dramatizes ■

the brutality and the evil of the white man against defenseless blacks. And in the racial climate of this country today, it is anybody's guess which of the "extremes" in approach to the black man's problems might *personally* meet a fatal catastrophe first—"non-violent" Dr. King, or so-called "violent" me.

Starting Time	
Reading Time	
Finishing Time	
Reading Rate	

COMPREHENSION —

Read the following questions and statements. For each one, put an X in the box before the option that contains the most complete or accurate answer.

1. As a child, Malcolm X was exposed to the teachings of
   ☐ a. Marcus Garvey.
   ☐ b. Booker T. Washington.
   ☐ c. Stokely Carmichael.
   ☐ d. Dr. Martin Luther King, Jr.

2. Malcolm X experienced major problems in building his all-black organization because
   ☐ a. people remembered his earlier attitudes.
   ☐ b. innovators are subject to criticism.
   ☐ c. idealism is often met with cynicism.
   ☐ d. white-black brotherhood is an unrealistic objective.

3. In paragraph 10 of this selection, the organization used is one of
   ☐ a. time order.
   ☐ b. cause and effect.
   ☐ c. true comparisons.
   ☐ d. statistical evidence.

4. In order for black people to institute change in America, Malcolm X felt there must be
   ☐ a. unity in their own ranks.
   ☐ b. more educated blacks.
   ☐ c. common religious values among mankind.
   ☐ d. less violent action against whites.

5. The careful reader will conclude that Malcolm X was
   ☐ a. a black racist.
   ☐ b. a developing personality.
   ☐ c. an Oriental mystic.
   ☐ d. an advocate of violence.

6. Malcolm X's statement that anger can blind human vision is
   ☐ a. disillusioned.
   ☐ b. sophisticated.
   ☐ c. foolish.
   ☐ d. honest.

7. Malcolm X saw the black man of his time as lacking
   ☐ a. money.
   ☐ b. racial dignity.
   ☐ c. leadership.
   ☐ d. religious values.

8. The tone of the selection can be classified as
   ☐ a. aggressive.
   ☐ b. sorrowful.
   ☐ c. thoughtful.
   ☐ d. angry.

9. Malcolm X's personality in this article is relatively
   ☐ a. calm and peaceful.
   ☐ b. incoherent.
   ☐ c. questioning.
   ☐ d. unconcerned.

10. The repetition of the word "sincere" in this selection is used to
    - ☐ a. enhance description.
    - ☐ b. express remorse.
    - ☐ c. emphasize a point.
    - ☐ d. create a metaphor.

Comprehension Skills

1. recalling specific facts
2. retaining concepts
3. organizing facts
4. understanding the main idea
5. drawing a conclusion
6. making a judgment
7. making an inference
8. recognizing tone
9. understanding characters
10. appreciating literary forms

VOCABULARY, PART TWO—

Write the term that makes the most sense in each sentence.

solidarity   ~~instill~~
~~incentive~~   arrogance
~~complacency~~

1. Malcolm X felt people needed a(n)

   _____ to motivate themselves

   to change their lives.

2. He feared that they would settle into

   _____ and be willing to accept

   things as they were.

3. He proposed that there was a need for

   _____ among blacks, a will-

   ingness to stand together for change.

4. He wanted to _____ a sense of

   pride into black people.

5. This pride would not be based on

   _____ , but rather on a quiet

   sort of self-confidence.

agnostics   hovering
subtly   conjunction
smugness

6. Malcolm X told whites that they could work in

   _____ with blacks, but they

   couldn't actually join black organizations.

7. He felt that some whites were just

   _____ around when they could

   be actively working in their own communities.

8. Then these whites would often develop a(n)

   _____ about how good and

   helpful they were.

9. In reality, Malcolm X felt that the whites' pres-

   ence—not directly, but _____

   —made black organizations less effective.

10. Christians and Jews, believers and

    _____ —all could do their

    own part among their own people.

Comprehension Score   ☐

Vocabulary Score   ☐

WRITING—

Malcolm X is regarded by many today as one of the great black leaders. What signs of his greatness do you see in this selection? Write a few paragraphs explaining how the selection shows important beliefs and ideas that Malcolm X had.

STUDY SKILLS—

Read the following passage and answer the questions that follow it.

Editing Your Work, II

Make sure to check every sentence in themes you write. Many problems in a theme or essay may be found in the sentence structure.

3. Check Punctuation. Punctuation is intended to help the reader understand your writing. It is a way of showing on paper the pauses and inflections made in speech.

4. Check Pronouns. Pronouns replace nouns. The antecedent to every pronoun must be clear to the reader. There should be no doubt what every "it," "he," "they," or "him" refers to.

Check, too, to be sure that each pronoun agrees with its antecedent in person and number. A frequent error is to use a plural pronoun (these, they) to replace a singular noun.

5. Improve Nouns and Verbs. Many times a writer will use the same nouns and verbs over and over. This makes the writing dull and unimaginative. Decide whether each important noun and verb in your paper needs to be replaced with a more specific and expressive word. Help the reader see and feel your thoughts. However, avoid artificial or over-inflated language. The object is to produce impact, not poetry.

6. Add Adjectives. Sometimes sentences can be improved by adding a well-chosen adjective. Try it; it often works. Practice doing this with simple sentences and see how interesting they can become. But be careful; some-times a simple, unadorned statement is best, depending on the effect you are trying to create.

1. Punctuation helps the reader to

    _____ your writing.

2. A frequent error in writing is to use a plural pronoun

    to replace a _____ noun.

3. Help the reader to see and

    _____ your thoughts through

    your writing.

4. Sentences can sometimes be improved by adding a

    _____ adjective.

5. In Malcolm X's statement, "... my voice helped to

    save America from a grave, possibly even a fatal,

    catastrophe," the adjectives *grave* and *fatal* give

    added impact to the noun _____.

4 | Philosophy and Opinions

Marcus Garvey

AUTHOR NOTES—

Born in Jamaica in 1887, Marcus Garvey learned firsthand about poor conditions for black people when he worked as a timekeeper on a plantation.

In 1914, Garvey founded the Universal Negro Improvement Association (UNIA), which was designed to improve the situation of black people worldwide. He also began a Back-to-Africa movement, based on the idea that blacks would not be free until they had a nation of their own, and that they should consider Africa their rightful home. Garvey moved the UNIA to the United States in 1916. At its peak of popularity, the organization boasted, by some estimates, three million followers. Garvey published *Negro World*, *Black Man*, and the two-volume *Philosophy and Opinions of Marcus Garvey*. He spent his later years in London, where he died in 1940.

VOCABULARY, PART ONE—

All of these terms are in the story you are about to read. Study each term and its meaning. Then answer the questions below.

As you read the story, notice how each vocabulary term is used. You will have more questions about the terms later.

deterring, preventing or discouraging

maligned, spoke ill of

unscrupulous, without principles or conscience

avail, aid; help

rendered, made

spurn, reject; treat with scorn

maltreated, treated badly

mire, mud; slime

sovereign, having supreme power or authority

connive, scheme; plot

1. Which word tells what two people do when they work out a secret plan to get rich quickly? _____

2. Which word tells what you did to a friend if you told mean stories about her behind her back? _____

3. Which word describes a person who would cheat his mother to get what he wanted?

    _____

4. If you are stopping someone from doing something wrong, what are you doing?

    _____

5. Which word could describe what an open field looks like after three straight days of rain? _____

A READING PURPOSE —

This selection explains Garvey's beliefs about how blacks should gain pride and confidence in themselves. As you read it, look for ideas that later black leaders also used in inspiring their audiences.

THE FUTURE AS I SEE IT

1   It comes to the individual, the race, the nation, once in a life time to decide upon the course to be pursued as a career. The hour has now struck for the individual Negro as well as the entire race to decide the course that will be pursued in the interest of our own liberty.

2   We who make up the Universal Negro Improvement Association have decided that we shall go forward, upward and onward toward the great goal of human liberty. We have determined among ourselves that all barriers placed in the way of our progress must be removed, must be cleared away for we desire to see the light of a brighter day.

The Negro Is Ready

3   The Universal Negro Improvement Association for five years has been proclaiming to the world the readiness of the Negro to carve out a pathway for himself in the course of life. Men of other races and nations have become alarmed at this attitude of the Negro in his desire to do things for himself and by himself. This alarm has become so universal that organizations have been brought into being here, there and everywhere for the purpose of <u>deterring</u> and obstructing this forward move of our race. Propaganda has been waged here, there and everywhere for the purpose of misinterpreting the intention of this organization; some have said that this organization seeks to create discord and discontent among the races; some say we are organized for the purpose of hating other people. Every sensible, sane and honest-minded person knows that the Universal Negro Improvement Association has no such intention. We are organized for the absolute purpose of bettering our condition, industrially, commercially, socially, religiously and politically. We are organized not to hate other men, but to lift ourselves, and to demand respect of all humanity. We have a program that we believe to be righteous; we believe it to be just, and we have made up our minds to lay down ourselves on the altar of sacrifice for the realization of this great hope of ours, based upon the foundation of righteousness. We declare to the world that Africa must be free, that the entire Negro race must be emancipated from industrial bondage, peonage and serfdom; we make no compromise, we make no apology in this our declaration. We do not desire to create offense on the part of other races, but we are determined that we shall be heard, that we shall be given the rights to which we are entitled.

The Propaganda of Our Enemies

4   For the purpose of creating doubts about the work of the Universal Negro Improvement Association, many attempts have been made to cast shadow and

gloom over our work. They have even written the most uncharitable things about our organization; they have spoken so unkindly of our effort, but what do we care? They spoke unkindly and uncharitably about all the reform movements that have helped in the betterment of humanity. They maligned the great movement of the Christian religion; they maligned the great liberation movements of America, of France, of England, of Russia; can we expect, then, to escape being maligned in this, our desire for the liberation of Africa and the freedom of four hundred million Negroes of the world?

5 We have unscrupulous men and organizations working in opposition to us. Some trying to capitalize the new spirit that has come to the Negro to make profit out of it to their own selfish benefit; some are trying to set back the Negro from seeing the hope of his own liberty, and thereby poisoning our people's mind against the motives of our organization; but every sensible far-seeing Negro in this enlightened age knows what propaganda means. It is the medium of discrediting that which you are opposed to, so that the propaganda of our enemies will be of little avail as soon as we are rendered able to carry to our peoples scattered throughout the world the true message of our great organization.

"Crocodiles" as Friends

6 Men of the Negro race, let me say to you that a greater future is in store for us; we have no cause to lose hope, to become faint-hearted. We must realize that upon ourselves depend our destiny, our future; we must carve out that future, that destiny, and we who make up the Universal Negro Improvement Association have pledged ourselves that nothing in the world shall stand in our way, nothing in the world shall discourage us, but opposition shall make us work harder, shall bring us closer together so that as one man the millions of us will march on toward that goal that we have set for ourselves. The new Negro shall not be deceived. The new Negro refuses to take advice from anyone who has not felt with him, and suffered with him. We have suffered for three hundred years, therefore we feel that the time has come when only those who have suffered with us can interpret our feelings and our spirit. It takes the slave to interpret the feelings of the slave; it takes the unfortunate man to interpret the spirit of his unfortunate brother; and so it takes the suffering Negro to interpret the spirit of his comrade. It is strange that so many people are interested in the Negro now, willing to advise him how to

In 1916, Marcus Garvey issued this statement of readiness and determination, anticipating much of the black rhetoric of decades to come.

act, and what organizations he should join, yet nobody was interested in the Negro to the extent of not making him a slave for two hundred and fifty years, reducing him to industrial peonage and serfdom after he was freed; it is strange that the same people can be so interested in the Negro now, as to tell him what organization he should follow and what leader he should support.

7 Whilst we are bordering on a future of brighter things, we are also at our danger period, when we must either accept the right philosophy, or go down by following deceptive propaganda which has hemmed us in for many centuries.

Deceiving the People

8 There is many a leader of our race who tells us that everything is well, and that all things will work out themselves and that a better day is coming. Yes, all of us know that a better day is coming; we all know that one day we will go home to Paradise, but whilst we are hoping by our Christian virtues to have an entry into Paradise we also realize that we are living on earth, and that the things that are practiced in Paradise are not practiced here. You have to treat this world as the world treats you; we are living in a temporal, material age, an age of activity, an age of racial, national selfishness. What else can you expect but to give back to the world what the world gives to you, and we are calling upon the four hundred million Negroes of the world to take a decided stand, a determined stand, that we shall occupy a firm position; that position shall be an emancipated race and a free nation of our own. We are determined that we shall have a free country; we are determined that we shall have a flag; we are determined that we shall have a government second to none in the world.

An Eye for an Eye

9 Men may spurn the idea, they may scoff at it; the metropolitan press of this country may deride us; yes, white men may laugh at the idea of Negroes talking about government; but let me tell you there is going to be a government, and let me say to you also that whatsoever you give, in like measure it shall be returned to you. The world is sinful, and

therefore man believes in the doctrine of an eye for an eye, a tooth for a tooth. Everybody believes that revenge is God's, but at the same time we are men, and revenge sometimes springs up, even in the most Christian heart.

10 Why should man write down a history that will react against him? Why should man perpetrate deeds of wickedness upon his brother which will return to him in like measure? Yes, the Germans <u>maltreated</u> the French in the Franco-Prussian war of 1870, but the French got even with the Germans in 1918. It is history, and history will repeat itself. Beat the Negro, brutalize the Negro, kill the Negro, burn the Negro, imprison the Negro, scoff at the Negro, deride the Negro, it may come back to you one of these fine days, because the supreme destiny of man is in the hands of God. God is no respecter of persons, whether that person be white, yellow or black. Today the one race is up, tomorrow it has fallen; today the Negro seems to be the footstool of the other races and nations of the world; tomorrow the Negro may occupy the highest rung of the great human ladder.

11 But, when we come to consider the history of man, was not the Negro a power, was he not great once? Yes, honest students of history can recall the day when Egypt, Ethiopia and Timbuctoo towered in their civilizations, towered above Europe, towered above Asia. When Europe was inhabited by a race of cannibals, a race of savages, naked men, heathens and pagans, Africa was peopled with a race of cultured black men, who were masters in art, science and literature; men who were cultured and refined; men who, it was said, were like the gods. Even the great poets of old sang in beautiful sonnets of the delight it afforded the gods to be in companionship with the Ethiopians. Why, then, should we lose hope? Black men, you were once great; you shall be great again. Lose not courage, lose not faith, go forward. The thing to do is to get organized; keep separated and you will be exploited, you will be robbed, you will be killed. Get organized, and you will compel the world to respect you. If the world fails to give you consideration, because you are black men, because you are Negroes, four hundred

millions of you shall, through organization, shake the pillars of the universe and bring down creation, even as Samson brought down the temple upon his head and upon the heads of the Philistines.

An Inspiring Vision

12 So Negroes, I say, through the Universal Negro Improvement Association, that there is much to live for. I have a vision of the future, and I see before me a picture of a redeemed Africa, with her dotted cities, with her beautiful civilization, with her millions of happy children, going to and fro. Why should I lose hope, why should I give up and take a back place in this age of progress? Remember that you are men, that God created you Lords of this creation. Lift up yourselves, men, take yourselves out of the <u>mire</u> and hitch your hopes to the stars; yes, rise as high as the very stars themselves. Let no man pull you down, let no man destroy your ambition, because man is but your companion, your equal; man is your brother; he is not your lord; he is not your <u>sovereign</u> master.

13 We of the Universal Negro Improvement Association feel happy; we are cheerful. Let them <u>connive</u> to destroy us; let them organize to destroy us; we shall fight the more. Ask me personally the cause of my success, and I say opposition; oppose me, and I fight the more, and if you want to find out the sterling worth of the Negro, oppose him, and under the leadership of the Universal Negro Improvement Association he shall fight his way to victory, and in the days to come, and I believe not far distant, Africa shall reflect a splendid demonstration of the worth of the Negro, of the determination of the Negro, to set himself free and to establish a government of his own.

Starting Time	
Reading Time	
Finishing Time	
Reading Rate	

COMPREHENSION —

Read the following questions and statements. For each one, put an X in the box before the option that contains the most complete or accurate answer.

1. The author defines propaganda as
   - ☐ a. a way of discrediting the opposition.
   - ☐ b. a white dominated press.
   - ☐ c. the use of violence to achieve goals.
   - ☐ d. the use of argument to convince the opposition.

2. The Universal Negro Improvement Association represents
   - ☐ a. South African blacks.
   - ☐ b. blacks of the world.
   - ☐ c. Ethiopians.
   - ☐ d. black Americans.

3. Garvey organizes his selection by using
   - ☐ a. charts.
   - ☐ b. subheadings.
   - ☐ c. personal experience.
   - ☐ d. numerical facts.

4. Which of the following best expresses the main idea of the selection?
   - ☐ a. The black race must unite and take its just place among the nations of the world.
   - ☐ b. It is the black man's right to demand an eye for an eye.
   - ☐ c. The UNIA must be guided by its Christian heritage.
   - ☐ d. Historically, liberation movements have always met with opposition.

5. UNIA members have vowed to
   - ☐ a. seek justice through the courts.
   - ☐ b. reject advice that is counter to their aims.
   - ☐ c. shun white influence wherever it is found.
   - ☐ d. meet violence with violence.

6. Black people have a right to be proud because of their
   - ☐ a. intellectual ability.
   - ☐ b. leadership qualities.
   - ☐ c. creative spirit.
   - ☐ d. great heritage.

7. "Crocodile" friends are
   - ☐ a. optimistic about the future.
   - ☐ b. people who believe in integration.
   - ☐ c. people who are interested in life in Africa.
   - ☐ d. people who like to give advice.

8. The tone suggested by the paragraph on "deceiving the people" is
   - ☐ a. sarcastic.
   - ☐ b. realistic.
   - ☐ c. prophetic.
   - ☐ d. poetic.

9. Which of the following best describes Marcus Garvey?
   - ☐ a. immoral
   - ☐ b. versatile
   - ☐ c. superficial
   - ☐ d. committed

10. When Garvey mentions the history of the Negro, he is appealing to black people's sense of
    - ☐ a. fairness.
    - ☐ b. pride.
    - ☐ c. kindness.
    - ☐ d. humor.

Comprehension Skills

1. recalling specific facts
2. retaining concepts
3. organizing facts
4. understanding the main idea
5. drawing a conclusion
6. making a judgment
7. making an inference
8. recognizing tone
9. understanding characters
10. appreciating literary forms

VOCABULARY, PART TWO —

Write the term that makes the most sense in each sentence.

deterring   **maligned**
spurn   **mire**
sovereign

1. Garvey felt that rather than being praised by whites, blacks were usually

   _____ by them.

2. Rather than helping blacks succeed, whites typically worked at _____ their progress.

3. Rather than wanting blacks to rise to new heights, many whites were content to let them wallow in the _____ .

4. But Garvey knew that whites should not be _____ rulers over blacks; he knew they should not be in charge of everything.

5. Blacks should _____ the attempts of whites to control them rather than passively accept these attempts.

unscrupulous   avail
rendered   maltreated
connive

6. Garvey knew that there were _____ men who didn't care if they treated blacks badly.

7. These men would plot and _____ to make things hard for blacks.

8. Garvey believed that when blacks were _____ , they should demand to be treated better.

9. Their complaints would be of little _____ , however, unless they were followed up by action.

10. By standing up for themselves, blacks would be _____ able to fight the battle against discrimination.

Comprehension Score [   ]

Vocabulary Score [   ]

W R I T I N G —
What ideas does Garvey present that are similar to those of Malcolm X? Write a few paragraphs explaining the similarities in their beliefs about what black people should do.

S T U D Y   S K I L L S —
Read the following passage and answer the questions that follow it.

Editing Your Work, III
7. Use Appropriate Language. There are, as you know, levels of language usage. Formal occasions demand the use of formal language, while conversations with friends permit the use of fragmented, informal speech. The language you use must be appropriate for your subject, purpose, and reader.

ANALYZE OTHER WRITING
The final bit of advice we can pass along to developing writers is to study the writings of others. By others, we refer, of course, to published authors and professional writers.

Most composition courses include the use of readers. These are books containing kinds and styles of writing for students to analyze and imitate. The selections in the reader are designed to serve as models for you.

Take a paragraph or two from an effective piece of writing and study it. Judge each sentence against the suggestions presented earlier for editing your work. Especially notice the nouns and verbs. Are they specific and image-provoking? They are certain to be in good writing.

Check the adjectives, too. See how experienced writers create word pictures through descriptive terms. Notice how the professionals organize their work and develop every idea.

Writing need not be a chore for you. Try following the suggestions given here, and see if you don't become a more expressive and more competent writer.

1. Different occasions demand different _____ of language usage.

2. Developing writers should study the work of _____ authors and professional writers.

3. Books known as readers, offered in composition courses, provide styles of writing for students to analyze and _____ .

4. Paragraph 4 of Garvey's essay, for example, could be studied for its alternating use of statements and

   _____ .

5. Professionals organize their work and

   _____ every idea.

5 I love those little booths at Benvenuti's

Gwendolyn Brooks

AUTHOR NOTES —

Gwendolyn Brooks was born in Topeka, Kansas, in 1917, but has spent much of her life in Chicago. She began writing as a child and has published numerous volumes of poetry as well as some prose. Brooks has been a lecturer or writing instructor at Columbia College and Northeastern Illinois University in Chicago and at the City College of New York and the University of Wisconsin. She has also been the poet laureate of Illinois and poetry consultant to the Library of Congress.

Brooks's first published book of poetry, *A Street in Bronzeville*, dealt with the everyday lives of people in a black Chicago neighborhood. Published in 1945, it was followed by *Annie Allen*, told from the point of view of a black city woman. For this volume Brooks received a Pulitzer Prize, making her the first black poet to receive that award. Others works include *The Bean Eaters; Selected Poems; Maud Martha*, her only novel; and *The Near-Johannasburg Boy* and *Winnie*.

VOCABULARY, PART ONE —

All of these terms are in the story you are about to read. Study each term and its meaning. Then answer the questions below.

As you read the story, notice how each vocabulary term is used. You will have more questions about the terms later.

dusky, somewhat dark in color

clamorous, noisy, boisterous

amorous, fond of making love

dissect, examine; analyze

ditty, catchy tune or jingle

carmine, deep red

cabana, vacation cottage near a beach

treasons, betrayals of some trust or duty

jester, person who amuses by acting like a fool

rationale, fundamental reason for something

1. Which word names a color? _____

2. Which word could name a short song used in a TV commercial?

    _____

3. Which word could you use in describing the shouting children playing out in the
    alley? _____

4. Which word might be used to name a statement explaining the whys and wherefores
    of some decision? _____

5. Which word might tell what you do when you take an engine apart and closely
    study its parts? _____

A READING PURPOSE —

In this poem Gwendolyn Brooks deals with the expectations of some visitors to a place
called Benvenuti's. Read to find out whether their expectations were met.

■

They get to Benvenuti's. There are booths
To hide in while observing tropical truths
About this—<u>dusky</u> folk, so <u>clamorous</u>!
So colorfully incorrect,
So <u>amorous</u>,
So flatly brave!
Boothed-in, one can detect,
<u>Dissect</u>.

One knows and scarcely knows what to expect.

What antics, knives, what lurching dirt; what <u>ditty</u>—
Dirty, rich, <u>carmine</u>, hot, not bottled up,
Straining in sexual soprano, cut
And praying in the bass, partial, unpretty.

They sit, sup,
(Whose friends, if not themselves, arrange
To rent in Venice "a very large <u>cabana</u>,
Small palace," and eat mostly what is strange.)
They sit, they settle; presently are met
By the light heat, the lazy upward whine
And lazy croaky downward drawl of "Tanya."
And their interiors sweat.

They lean back in the half-light, stab their stares
At: walls, panels of imitation oak
With would-be marbly look; linoleum squares
25 Of dusty rose and brown with little white splashes,
White curls; a vendor tidily encased;
Young yellow waiter moving with straight haste,
Old oaken waiter, lolling and amused;
Some paper napkins in a water glass;
30 Table, initialed, rubbed, as a desk in school.

They stare. They tire. They feel refused,
Feel overwhelmed by subtle <u>treasons</u>!
Nobody here will take the part of <u>jester</u>.

The absolute stutters, and the <u>rationale</u>
35 Stoops off in astonishment.
But not gaily
And not with their consent.

They play "They All Say I'm The Biggest Fool"
And "Voo Me On The Vot Nay" and "New Lester
40 Leaps In" and "For Sentimental Reasons."

But how shall they tell people they have been
Out Bronzeville way? For all the nickels in
Have not bought savagery or defined a "folk."

The colored people will not "clown."

45 The colored people arrive, sit firmly down,
Eat their Express Spaghetti, their T-bone steak,
Handling their steel and crockery with no clatter,
Laugh punily, rise, go firmly out of the door.

Starting Time	
Reading Time	
Finishing Time	
Reading Rate	

■

C O M P R E H E N S I O N —

Read the following questions and statements. For each one, put an X in the box before the option that contains the most complete or accurate answer.

1. Benvenuti's is a
   ☐ a. luxury hotel.
   ☐ b. lower-class hotel.
   ☐ c. nightclub.
   ☐ d. restaurant.

2. The people that the poem is mostly about are
   ☐ a. neighborhood blacks.
   ☐ b. neighborhood whites.
   ☐ c. blacks from out of the neighborhood.
   ☐ d. whites from out of the neighborhood.

3. The content of this poem involves
   ☐ a. one brief event.
   ☐ b. a series of events.
   ☐ c. a series of descriptions rather than an event.
   ☐ d. one event in the present and one in the past.

4. Which statement best summarizes this poem?
   ☐ a. There is no place more comfortable than a neighborhood hangout.
   ☐ b. Places are not always as people imagine them to be.
   ☐ c. Traveling around a city can bring people to some interesting places.
   ☐ d. Whites and blacks have very different diets.

5. The visitors to Benvenuti's have expected to find
   ☐ a. a T-bone steak at a fair price.
   ☐ b. a more up-to-date juke box.
   ☐ c. an exotic and exciting experience.
   ☐ d. an unusual stage show.

6. The description in lines 10–13 creates an impression of
   ☐ a. what the visitors imagine Benvenuti's to be like.
   ☐ b. what Benvenuti's is like at night.
   ☐ c. what Benvenuti's used to be like.
   ☐ d. what the general atmosphere of Bronzeville is like.

7. The visitors are upset because
   ☐ a. no one in Benvenuti's will pay much attention to them.
   ☐ b. the place and the people are different from what they imagined.
   ☐ c. they cannot see much from the booth they are sitting in.
   ☐ d. the "colored people" don't stay very long.

8. The tone of this poem is mostly
   ☐ a. matter-of-fact.
   ☐ b. angry.
   ☐ c. unconcerned.
   ☐ d. sarcastic.

9. The visitors to Benvenuti's
   ☐ a. are do-gooders trying to help out in the neighborhood.
   ☐ b. are people looking for a bargain.
   ☐ c. think they are superior to the regular customers.
   ☐ d. will probably be back again soon.

10. Brooks uses rhyme in this poem
   ☐ a. throughout, but not in a regular pattern.
   ☐ b. not at all.
   ☐ c. only occasionally.
   ☐ d. every two lines.

Comprehension Skills

1. recalling specific facts
2. retaining concepts
3. organizing facts
4. understanding the main idea
5. drawing a conclusion
6. making a judgment
7. making an inference
8. recognizing tone
9. understanding characters
10. appreciating literary forms

V O C A B U L A R Y ,   P A R T   T W O —

Write the term that makes the most sense in each sentence.

dusky   amorous
dissect   carmine
rationale

1. The visitors' _____ for going to Benvenuti's was to see something unusual.

2. They wanted to _____ each move of the regular customers in order to find out something about their lives.

3. Some expected the regulars to be

_____ , to hang all over each

other hugging and kissing.

4. The women there would wear

_____ lipstick and dress in

bright prints.

5. These _____ folks, so much

darker than they, must have exotic lives.

ditty   **cabana**
treasons   **jester**
clamorous

6. But no one at Benvenuti's was noisy and

_____ .

7. No one made them laugh by playing the role of

_____ .

8. A new _____ on the jukebox

was the most exciting thing they heard.

9. It was the regulars' duty to be unusual, the visitors

thought, and they were committing

_____ by just being ordinary.

10. Maybe staying at a _____

near the lake could bring some excitement to the

visitors' lives.

Comprehension Score ☐

Vocabulary Score ☐

W R I T I N G —

Is there a place in your neighborhood, or in a neighborhood you know of, that attracts visitors from out of the
area? Write a few paragraphs describing the place and explaining why you think people want to go there.

S T U D Y   S K I L L S —

Read the following passage and answer the questions
that follow it.

The Art of Writing, I

It seems that many students distinctly dislike writing, although reading, writing, and speaking are the learning
student's tools. We all have good ideas—the trouble aris-
es in expressing our ideas. It is lack of organization that
makes many students fear writing. Students who can organize their approach to writing will find the experience
rewarding if not enjoyable.

Here are the steps to follow when preparing to write:

1. State a Subject. You must think first and carefully
about your subject. A subject is more than a one-word
title; it should be a statement of the topic you plan to
discuss and should also make clear what you plan to say
about it. You should be able to state clearly in a sentence or two the views you wish to present relating to
your subject. Many students fail before they even begin
by not knowing what their views are. Obviously, you cannot write intelligently if you don't know what you are
going to say. Spend enough time forming your subject
statement; it saves you time later.

2. Limit the Subject. You should know before you
begin writing how long your paper is to be, or how long
you want it to be. This means that you will have to limit
your subject to just those aspects that can be adequately
covered in a paper of that length. If you try to include
too much in too little space, the result will be that you
will not have really covered anything. Your paper will
consist of a series of unrelated, general facts with no real
point or substance.

You must stop, think, and define the limitations of
your subject. Decide exactly on the two or three points
you want to consider and know before you write what
you intend to say about them.

1. Students who can organize their

_____ to writing will find the

experience rewarding.

2. You should be able to state clearly, in a sentence or

two, the _____ you wish to

present relating to your subject.

3. Before Gwendolyn Brooks began her poem, for instance, she most likely knew that she wanted to describe both a place and the

   _____ who came to visit it.

4. If you spend enough time forming your subject

   _____ , you will save yourself

   time later.

5. You must stop, think, and define the

   _____ of your subject.

Why I Ran Away

Bloke Modisane

AUTHOR NOTES—
Actor, journalist, and author William "Bloke" Modisane was a black South African intellectual who used his stage performances and writings to dramatize the plight of South African blacks living under apartheid. Born in a Johannesburg suburb in 1923, Modisane lived there until 1958 when the government bulldozed the entire suburb—saying it was too close to neighboring white areas. He left Africa in 1958 and became an actor in Britain, appearing in several politically controversial plays. Modisane's work includes many plays, several collections of verse, and his autobiography, all written under his pen name Bloke. Modisane died in Dortmund, West Germany, in 1986.

VOCABULARY, PART ONE—
All of these terms are in the story you are about to read. Study each term and its meaning. Then answer the questions below.

As you read the story, notice how each vocabulary term is used. You will have more questions about the terms later.

rationalizations, justifications; excuses

allocated, distributed

concessions, acts of giving in; compromises

humane, kind; compassionate; charitable

maniacal, crazy; insane

avenues, ways of approach

stipulate, to specify in an agreement

euphemistically, using mild words instead of harsh, direct ones

indict, charge with an offense or crime

apartheid, the South African system of absolute separation of the races

1. Which word could describe how you were speaking if you called someone "dearly departed" rather than "dead"? _____

2. Which word is associated with an activity done by a court?

_____

3. Which word could describe a friend who always tries to help people down on their luck? _____

4. Which word could describe a person who stands on the street corner and screams wild insults at passers-by? _____

5. Which word could describe what a father did who distributed his land evenly among his three children? _____

A READING PURPOSE—

This selection describes some of the laws and conditions that made living in apartheid South Africa intolerable. As you read, note the many restrictions that were placed on blacks by the government.

---

1 When all the facts have been examined, the motives analyzed, the <u>rationalizations</u> equated, I still have to face my guilty conscience, my color and the commitment to fight the prejudices against it. And nagging at the back of my mind persists this confrontation: Were you not running away in deciding to leave South Africa? The fact is, I ran away. I am a coward. False heroics and rationalizations are unnecessary.

2 South Africa is a pigmentocracy, dedicated before God and the whole world to the proposition that "South Africa is the white man's country: it shall never be ruled by Kaffirs, Hottentots and coolies." White is right, and to be black is to be despised, dehumanized, classed among the beasts, hounded and persecuted, discriminated against, segregated and oppressed by government and by man's greed. White is the positive standard, black is the negative. Symbols of wealth, prestige and authority are <u>allocated</u> to the whites; and inferiority, humiliation and servitude are the lot of the black man. The society is divided into groups of "haves" and "have-nots." The "haves" want to keep on having and to see to it that the "have-nots" work for them.

3 Although the whites have their ideological differences, they are united in the broader concept of maintaining white supremacy and the furtherance of that state. There is a vital but small number of liberal South Africans who believed in a shared society with more <u>concessions</u> made to the Africans, who contend that race legislations should be more <u>humane</u>, just and Christian. They believe in the gradual integration of "responsible" Africans into the social, economic and political life of South Africa.

4 Under normal conditions, with a show of faith, this could be acceptable to the responsible Africans. But the responsible African is a despised figurehead, and the reality lies in the recognition and acceptance of the irresponsible African, who does not want his freedom on the never-never scheme, but wants it now. This irresponsible African is the one to be reckoned with—while there is still time.

5 He is impatient, militant and a revolutionary. He is obsessed with freedom—that it is his historical right. He resents being told that as soon as power rests in his hands the minority races, the whites, will be oppressed. This I find fascinating. Why do these minority races believe that they have a moral right to oppress the Africans, when they, in turn, fear oppression directed toward them? Do they hold a world patent? The African knows what it is like to be oppressed—he is preoccupied with canceling it and stamping it out from the face of the world. Oppression is not an expression of his life.

6 During moments of bitterness I have been known to blurt out that white South Africans need to be made to live through the humiliation of oppression, to be made to realize its total inhumanity. But oppression is something that cannot be wished on even one's enemies. This is what is so terrifying about being black in South Africa, this <u>maniacal</u> desire to revenge, but even more terrifying is the reality that the white South African, who counts, is determined to maintain the system. Denying the African all the civilized means, not only to change the system but even to protest against it in a democratic manner.

7 All the <u>avenues</u> of moral protest have been blockaded by legislation like the Natives (Prohibition of Interdicts) Act of 1956, by which the governor general can, by proclamation, order an African to leave a certain area. This the African must do, and no court of law may grant an interdict preventing such summary endorsement or an appeal for a stay or suspension of the removal order: this even if it is established as a fact that the order was intended for someone else and was served in error. The provisions of the Natives Labor (Settlement of Disputes) Act of 1953 <u>stipulate</u> that it is unlawful for an African to go on strike. He becomes liable, on conviction, to imprisonment for three years, to a maximum fine of £500, or a combination of the two. The Public Safety Act of 1953 empowers the governor general, or under special conditions the minister of justice, to authorize, by proclamation, any police constable to arrest any person and imprison him without trial. This state of emergency may be invoked whenever the authorities hold that the safety of the public is endangered and the ordinary law is inadequate.

8 <u>Euphemistically</u> there is freedom of speech in South Africa, enjoyed in equal measure by all, even the African, so long as it is not used to criticize the government's racial policy. The Suppression of Communism Act makes such criticisms a treasonable offense. This Act enables anybody to be labeled a Communist who asserts that any form of government which withholds from a people the basic human rights is wrong and must be abolished. I believe that South Africa is a tyranny, that the system should be smashed—if not by moral protest, then by force. And so I have finally done it; I have committed treason against the legally constituted government of the state.

9 All these acts and prohibitions almost drove me to the point of being insensitive to oppression. I carried a pass because it was law, lived in a segregated location, used the "Natives Only" entrances into public buildings, used the "Natives and Goods" lifts, walked over to "Native Counters" in the post office and the bank, used the green "For Colored Persons Only" buses and allowed myself to be segregated and barely tolerated in the Indian-owned cinemas.

A victim of apartheid writes with uneasy heart and mind from self-imposed exile.

10 I locked myself up in my room to have that illegal drink, bowed to the Immorality Act of 1957, which lays down that sexual acts between black and whites are illegal, immoral and un-Christian. I permitted my labor to be exploited because I had to live. I accepted the discrimination against my skin as a physical reality I had to live with; accommodated myself to the humiliation of labels like "John" or "Jim" or "Boy" without strongly protesting. I stood by while a sidewalk bully pushed his finger into my nostril, spitting insults at me. Stood there suffocating with anger, afraid that any moment I was going to shout "Go to hell!" Restraining my fingers from closing round his throat and squeezing.

11 Then against my impulses would rise the voice of discretion: "Don't do it! You must not lose your temper. It's not worth it, bide your time." I would know the wisdom of it, and in the face of the gathered crowd I would apologize appropriately, plead with the white bully not to strike me. Some white gallants would smile acknowledgingly and the women would be sympathetic and advise me to go home, John.

12 I could not live with it any longer. I knew that I had to run, or lose my temper and even my sanity. I was not a dedicated platform politician, not even a member of the African National Congress. I was blinded by the violence of the oppression and could not reconcile my feelings with the ANC policy of nonviolence in the face of violence. The situation became unbearable to me as an individual. I felt stifled, unable to express and fulfill myself as an individual man. I felt the relentless inevitability of the clash, the direct immediacy of blood, in the resolving of the South African riddle. The prospect terrified me as I began to see this as the realism to which Africans are being driven. Because I am a coward, because I love humanity more than I hate oppression, I could not stay to face the possibility of slitting throats. I hate all violence, mental and physical, and no rationalization can cease its stark

horror: I am a moral coward who cannot take a gun and go to war.

13 I know that the riddle of South Africa will have to be resolved in South Africa, perhaps without blood. But the possibility of bloodshed cannot be brushed aside, and I hope that through my writing I can yet make the world realize the danger gathering in the Union. That what will happen there will touch the rest of the world. For the world outside is responsible for the furtherance and continuance of the system. I indict the world. Every investment, every gold bar bought from South Africa helps to pay for the machinery of apartheid. ■

Starting Time ☐

Reading Time ☐

Finishing Time ☐

Reading Rate ☐

COMPREHENSION —

Read the following questions and statements. For each one, put an X in the box before the option that contains the most complete or accurate answer.

1. According to Modisane, opposition to certain aspects of apartheid exists among some South African whites; however, all South African whites are committed to
   ☐ a. maintaining white supremacy.
   ☐ b. widening the racial gap.
   ☐ c. encouraging genocide.
   ☐ d. ignoring world opinion.

2. The author left South Africa
   ☐ a. to avoid a confrontation for which he was temperamentally unsuited.
   ☐ b. to protest the country's inhuman racial policies.
   ☐ c. to escape capture by a special unit created to enforce the Immorality Act of 1957.
   ☐ d. to further his literary career in an atmosphere free from the suffocating grip of apartheid.

3. In paragraphs 7–13, the writer presents the facts in a type of
   ☐ a. cause-and-effect relationship.
   ☐ b. time-order sequence.
   ☐ c. descending order.
   ☐ d. simple listing.

4. Which of the following gives the main thought of this selection?
   ☐ a. European merchants are not involved in South African politics.
   ☐ b. Responsible Africans are despised figureheads.
   ☐ c. White Africans believe in gradual integration.
   ☐ d. The apartheid system is well entrenched in South Africa.

5. The writer leads us to believe that the end result of apartheid will be
   ☐ a. acceptance.
   ☐ b. violence.
   ☐ c. integration.
   ☐ d. apathy.

6. In Modisane's eyes, responsible Africans are to irresponsible Africans as
   ☐ a. honest men are to criminals.
   ☐ b. conservatives are to liberals.
   ☐ c. conformists are to nonconformists.
   ☐ d. Uncle Toms are to militants.

7. According to the author, apartheid could be seriously threatened and possibly overcome by
   ☐ a. the Suppression of Communism Act.
   ☐ b. world economic sanctions.
   ☐ c. the African National Congress.
   ☐ d. Hottentots, Kaffirs, and coolies.

8. The tone of this selection is one of
   ☐ a. regret.
   ☐ b. sympathy.
   ☐ c. commitment.
   ☐ d. indecision.

9. Bloke Modisane can be described as
   ☐ a. a street fighter.
   ☐ b. a person willing to wait around for change.
   ☐ c. a man with no alternative but to run.
   ☐ d. an artist concerned only with his writing.

10. The selection is written in
    ☐ a. first person.
    ☐ b. second person.
    ☐ c. third person limited.
    ☐ d. third person omniscient.

Comprehension Skills

1. recalling specific facts
2. retaining concepts
3. organizing facts
4. understanding the main idea
5. drawing a conclusion
6. making a judgment
7. making an inference
8. recognizing tone
9. understanding characters
10. appreciating literary forms

VOCABULARY, PART TWO—
Write the term that makes the most sense in each sentence.

rationalizations   concessions
maniacal   avenues
apartheid

1. At one point Modisane had hoped that there were _____ through which South Africa could explore the question of equality for blacks.

2. But he soon learned that most white South Africans were so _____ about race that they could not act in a sane way.

3. Under the system of _____ , separation between the races in South Africa was absolute.

4. This system, Modisane believed, made it impossible for whites to give in and make _____ to blacks.

5. Some of these whites offered _____ excusing their behavior, but there was no real justification for their not wanting to share power.

stipulate   euphemistically
allocated   humane
indict

6. Not all white South Africans treated blacks badly; some behaved in a(n) _____ manner.

7. They wanted to see rights _____ fairly among all the people.

8. They believed laws should clearly _____ that blacks had equal rights.

9. But Modisane found reasons to _____ even these good-hearted people for some of their actions.

10. For instance, he became angry with people talking _____ about "the problem" instead of calling it what it was: racial hatred.

Comprehension Score [   ]

Vocabulary Score [   ]

WRITING —
Modisane's suggestion that other countries' refusal to do business in South Africa might help to overthrow the system turned out to be at least partially correct. Write a few paragraphs to express your ideas about why this kind of economic pressure would work to change a government.

STUDY SKILLS —

Read the following passage and answer the questions that follow it.

The Art of Writing, II

We have said that the first two tasks for the writer are (1) select a subject, and (2) limit the subject. Here are the next steps for the student to take.

3. Clarify the Purpose. Every student has a purpose in mind when writing. It may be the purpose assigned by the instructor or, too often, it may be some vague, poorly defined idea of what the student hopes to accomplish.

Writers must know clearly what their purpose in writing is: a position must be taken regarding the subject and the writer must defend or support it. Purposeless writing is ineffective writing. Unless readers know where you are leading them, your writing will not make sense. Aimless writing creates aimless and dull reading. Be sure of your stand before beginning to write.

4. Support the Ideas. Every paper, essay, or theme must do more than merely present facts: the facts must be supported. A writer cannot expect readers to accept a particular position unless it is properly presented and clearly explained.

This does not mean that everything you write has to take a stand on some controversial issue—it means that, whatever the subject and purpose, your writing must include facts, details, and illustrations that make your ideas reasonable and acceptable to the reader.

There are, of course, various patterns of development used by authors. As you read and study, take ideas from these patterns. Employ the different techniques shown through these patterns in your own writing. Observe how skilled writers flood the reader with all kinds of support for their generalizations and main ideas.

1. The first two tasks of the writer are to
   _____ a subject and to limit
   the subject.

2. The writer must take a _____
   regarding his subject and must defend or support it.

3. Unless the reader knows where you are leading him,
   your writing will not make _____.

4. Your writing must include facts, details, and illustrations that make your ideas reasonable and
   _____ to the reader.

5. Modisane's writing explains various laws in South
   Africa as illustrations of what made the system of
   _____ intolerable.

Atlanta Compromise Speech

Booker T. Washington

AUTHOR NOTES—

Booker T. Washington was the most influential black leader and educator of his time in the United States. Born a slave in 1856, he was freed by the U.S. government in 1865, and later attended the Hampton Institute, an industrial school for blacks and Native Americans in Virginia. Washington became a teacher at Hampton in 1879 and in 1881 founded the Tuskegee Institute, a vocational school for blacks in Alabama.

Washington believed that blacks could benefit more from a practical, vocational education than from a college education. He felt that if black people worked hard, acquired property, and developed a strong economic foundation, they would be granted civil and political rights. In keeping with his moderate political stance, Washington never publicly supported black political causes. He did, however, secretly finance lawsuits opposing segregation.

Washington's immensely popular autobiography, *Up From Slavery*, was published in 1901. He remained a powerful leader until his death in 1915.

VOCABULARY, PART ONE—

All of these terms are in the story you are about to read. Study each term and its meaning. Then answer the questions below.

As you read the story, notice how each vocabulary term is used. You will have more questions about the terms later.

afforded, offered

eloquent, expressing ideas clearly and beautifully

superficial, concerned only with the obvious; lacking in substance

fidelity, loyalty

treacherous, acting like a traitor; disloyal

curtail, cut short; put a stop to

retarding, delaying; hindering

philanthropists, people who donate large amounts of money to worthy causes

ostracized, excluded

animosities, strong dislikes; hostilities

1. Which word could describe a speech containing many beautiful comparisons and descriptions? _____

2. Which word could identify an organization of people who gave a local college $5 million for a new library? _____

3. Which word tells what you did when you refused to invite one member of your group to a party? _____

4. Which word could describe a conversation in which nothing was discussed in any seriousness or depth? _____

5. Which word tells what police would do to the flow of traffic if they totally blocked off a road? _____

A READING PURPOSE —

This selection makes clear Washington's specific ideas about how blacks in the South at the end of the 19th century could prosper. Read to find out what his ideas were.

MR. PRESIDENT AND GENTLEMEN OF THE BOARD OF DIRECTORS AND CITIZENS.

1 One-third of the population of the South is of the Negro race. No enterprise seeking the material, civil, or moral welfare of this section can disregard this element of our population and reach the highest success. I but convey to you, Mr. President and Directors, the sentiment of the masses of my race when I say that in no way have the value and manhood of the American Negro been more fittingly and generously recognized than by the managers of this magnificent Exposition at every stage of its progress. It is a recognition that will do more to cement the friendship of the two races than any occurrence since the dawn of our freedom.

2 Not only this, but the opportunity here <u>afforded</u> will awaken among us a new era of industrial progress. Ignorant and inexperienced, it is not strange that in the first years of our new life we began at the top instead of at the bottom; that a seat in Congress or the state legislature was more sought than real estate or industrial skill; that the political convention of stump speaking had more attractions than starting a dairy farm or truck garden.

3 A ship lost at sea for many days suddenly sighted a friendly vessel. From the mast of the unfortunate vessel was seen a signal, "Water, water; we die of thirst!" The answer from the friendly vessel at once came back, "Cast down your bucket where you are." A second time the signal, "Water, water; send us water!" ran up from the distressed vessel, and was answered, "Cast down your bucket where you are." And a third and fourth signal for water was answered, "Cast down your bucket where you are." The captain of the distressed vessel, at last heeding the injunction, cast down his bucket, and it came up full of fresh, sparkling water from the mouth of the Amazon River. To those of my race who depend on bettering their condition in a foreign land or who underestimate the importance of cultivating friendly relations with the Southern white man, who is their next-door neighbour, I would say: "Cast down your bucket where you are"—cast it down in making friends in every manly way of the people of all races by whom we are surrounded.

4 Cast it down in agriculture, mechanics, in commerce, in domestic service, and in the professions. And in this connection it is well to bear in mind that whatever other sins the South may be called to bear, when it comes to business, pure and simple, it is in the South that the Negro is given a man's chance in the commercial world, and in nothing is this Exposition more <u>eloquent</u> than in emphasizing this chance. Our greatest danger is that in the great leap from slavery to freedom we may overlook the

fact that the masses of us are to live by the productions of our hands, and fail to keep in mind that we shall prosper in proportion as we learn to dignify and glorify common labour and put brains and skill into the common occupations of life; shall prosper in proportion as we learn to draw the line between the superficial and the substantial, the ornamental gewgaws of life and the useful. No race can prosper till it learns that there is as much dignity in tilling a field as in writing a poem. It is at the bottom of life we must begin, and not at the top. Nor should we permit our grievances to overshadow our opportunities.

5   To those of the white race who look to the incoming of those of foreign birth and strange tongue and habits for the prosperity of the South, were I permitted I would repeat what I say to my own race, "Cast down your bucket where you are." Cast it down among the eight millions of Negroes whose habits you know, whose fidelity and love you have tested in days when to have proved treacherous meant the ruin of your firesides. Cast down your bucket among these people who have, without strikes and labour wars, tilled your fields, cleared your forests, built your railroads and cities, and brought forth treasures from the bowels of the earth, and helped make possible this magnificent representation of the progress of the South. Casting down your bucket among my people, helping and encouraging them as you are doing on these grounds, and to education of head, hand, and heart, you will find that they will buy your surplus land, make blossom the waste places in your fields, and run your factories. While doing this, you can be sure in the future, as in the past, that you and your families will be surrounded by the most patient, faithful, law-abiding, and unresentful people that the world has seen. As we have proved our loyalty to you in the past, in nursing your children, watching by the sick-bed of your mothers and fathers, and often following them with tear-dimmed eyes to their graves, so in the future, in our humble way, we shall stand by you with a devotion that no foreigner can approach, ready to lay down our lives, if need be, in defence of yours, interlacing our industrial, commercial, civil, and religious life with yours in a way that shall make the interests of both races one. In all things that are purely social we can be as separate as the fingers, yet one as the hand in all things essential to mutual progress.

6   There is no defence or security for any of us except in the highest intelligence and development of all.

If anywhere there are efforts tending to curtail the fullest growth of the Negro, let these efforts be turned into stimulating, encouraging, and making him the most useful and intelligent citizen. Effort or means so invested will pay a thousand per cent interest. These efforts will be twice blessed—"blessing him that gives and him that takes."

7   There is no escape through law of man or God from the inevitable:—

> The laws of changeless justice bind
> Oppressor with oppressed;
> And close as sin and suffering joined
> We march to fate abreast.

8   Nearly sixteen millions of hands will aid you in pulling the load upward, or they will pull against you the load downward. We shall constitute one-third and more of the ignorance and crime of the South, or one-third its intelligence and progress; we shall contribute one-third to the business and industrial prosperity of the South, or we shall prove a veritable body of death, stagnating, depressing, retarding every effort to advance the body politic.

9   Gentlemen of the Exposition, as we present to you our humble effort at an exhibition of our progress, you must not expect overmuch. Starting thirty years ago with ownership here and there in a few quilts and pumpkins and chickens (gathered from miscellaneous sources), remember the path that has led from these to the inventions and production of agricultural implements, buggies, steam-engines, newspapers, books, statuary, carving, paintings, the management of drugstores and banks, has not been trodden without contact with thorns and thistles. While we take pride in what we exhibit as a result of our independent efforts, we do not for a moment forget that our part in this exhibition would fall far short of your expectations but for the constant help that has come to our educational life, not only from the Southern states, but especially from Northern philanthropists, who have made their gifts a constant stream of blessing and encouragement.

10 The wisest among my race understand that the agitation of questions of social equality is the extremest folly, and that progress in the enjoyment of all the privileges that will come to us must be the result of severe and constant struggle rather than of artificial forcing. No race that has anything to con-

tribute to the markets of the world is long in any degree <u>ostracized</u>. It is important and right that all privileges of the law be ours, but it is vastly more important that we be prepared for the exercises of these privileges. The opportunity to earn a dollar in a factory just now is worth infinitely more than the opportunity to spend a dollar in an opera-house.

11 In conclusion, may I repeat that nothing in thirty years has given us more hope and encouragement, and drawn us so near to you of the white race, as this opportunity offered by the Exposition; and here bending, as it were, over the altar that represents the results of the struggles of your race and mine, both starting practically empty-handed three decades ago, I pledge that in your effort to work out the great and intricate problem which God has laid at the doors of the South, you shall have at all times the patient, sympathetic help of my race; only let this be constantly in mind, that, while

from representations in these buildings of the product of field, of forest, of mine, of factory, letters, and art, much good will come, yet far above and beyond material benefits will be that higher good, that, let us pray God, will come, in a blotting out of sectional differences and racial <u>animosities</u> and suspicions, in a determination to administer absolute justice, in a willing obedience among all classes to the mandates of law. This, this, coupled with our material prosperity, will bring into our beloved South a new heaven and a new earth.

Starting Time	
Reading Time	
Finishing Time	
■ Reading Rate	

COMPREHENSION —

Read the following questions and statements. For each one, put an X in the box before the option that contains the most complete or accurate answer.

1. According to this article, what percentage of the Southern population is black?
   - ☐ a. one-third
   - ☐ b. one-half
   - ☐ c. three-quarters
   - ☐ d. seven-eighths

2. Washington praised the directors of the Exposition because
   - ☐ a. they had allowed him to address their assembly.
   - ☐ b. they acknowledged the contributions of black people to the South.
   - ☐ c. one-third of the Exposition's labor force was black.
   - ☐ d. he feared censure and retaliation from certain powerful groups.

3. To show that opportunities may be open to black people, Washington uses
   - ☐ a. a biographical sketch.
   - ☐ b. similes.
   - ☐ c. a fable.
   - ☐ d. an unsolved problem.

4. Washington favored a temporary form of segregation because he
   - ☐ a. did not believe that blacks could compete equally on a social basis.
   - ☐ b. was addressing a white audience in a white stronghold.
   - ☐ c. believed it would eventually disappear if blacks made themselves economically indispensable.
   - ☐ d. could not tolerate social protest and civil rights agitation.

5. In Washington's statement that "...we can be as separate as the fingers, yet one as the hand...," he is telling his white audience that
   - ☐ a. blacks are striving for total integration.
   - ☐ b. blacks will contribute economically but will not compete socially.
   - ☐ c. progress is uppermost in the minds of black people.
   - ☐ d. education will eventually dispel present fears.

6. In Washington's view, status for the black race may be obtained through
   ☐ a. economic sanctions.
   ☐ b. persistent aggression.
   ☐ c. forced integration.
   ☐ d. hard work and patience.

7. The "higher good" referred to in the conclusion of this address is
   ☐ a. a black commitment to unity.
   ☐ b. cooperation and prosperity.
   ☐ c. hope and charity.
   ☐ d. protection under the law for all classes of society.

8. The tone of this speech is
   ☐ a. liberal.
   ☐ b. conservative.
   ☐ c. radical.
   ☐ d. self-righteous.

9. Booker T. Washington was
   ☐ a. openly bitter.
   ☐ b. poorly educated.
   ☐ c. accommodating to whites.
   ☐ d. delightfully witty.

10. The phrase "Cast down your bucket where you are" in the selection shows an effective use of
   ☐ a. exaggeration.
   ☐ b. repetition.
   ☐ c. personification.
   ☐ d. irony.

Comprehension Skills

1. recalling specific facts
2. retaining concepts
3. organizing facts
4. understanding the main idea
5. drawing a conclusion
6. making a judgment
7. making an inference
8. recognizing tone
9. understanding characters
10. appreciating literary forms

VOCABULARY, PART TWO—

Write the term that makes the most sense in each sentence.

fidelity   **retarding**
philanthropists   **afforded**
ostracized

1. Washington felt that the Cotton States Exposition _____ Southern blacks an opportunity to show what they could do.

2. He was grateful to the _____ who had donated money to help his people.

3. He knew that in the past blacks had been _____ , so he was particularly happy that they were included in the Exposition.

4. He asked for help in removing the obstacles that had been _____ blacks' progress.

5. He said that in return for their belief in his people, the whites would be repaid by the blacks' _____ .

eloquent   **superficial**
treacherous   **curtail**
animosities

6. Washington hoped that the whites approved of his people and had put aside their past _____ .

7. He believed that they were interested in blacks' progress and would not try to _____ it.

8. He was confident that whites would not turn their backs on blacks or perform other _____ acts.

9. Washington was a good speaker and expressed his ideas in a(n) _____ manner.

10. His ideas were not _____ ; he had thought them through carefully and in some depth.

Comprehension Score [ ]

Vocabulary Score [ ]

Reaction papa w/ Video

W R I T I N G —

How do you think his white audience responded to Washington's speech? What do you think they thought of him? Write a few paragraphs expressing your opinion. Back up what you say by referring to specific things Washington says.

S T U D Y   S K I L L S —

Read the following passage and answer the questions that follow it.

The Art of Writing, III

The first four steps in organizing a piece of writing are (1) state a subject, (2) limit the subject, (3) clarify the purpose, and (4) support the ideas. The next steps are the following.

5. Distinguish Fact from Opinion. In every essay or theme, the writer presents both facts and opinions regarding the subject. Students whose writing approach is disorganized frequently fail to identify for the reader which of their ideas are facts and which are opinions. As one would expect, this leaves the reader hanging and confused—uncertain as to the validity of the writer's conclusions.

Present the facts clearly for your reader to see and understand. Then state opinions based on those facts for the reader to appraise and evaluate. The reader can then intelligently decide whether to agree or disagree with you. This is an instance of effective communication at work.

6. Structure the Presentation. A writer's organization must be clear to the reader; the reader must be able to see how a theme or essay is structured. Unstructured writing is disorganized—the reader does not know where you are leading and is unable to see the logic of your discussion. The reader needs to be aware of the divisions in a subject—when one aspect of a discussion is completed and another is introduced. The reader also needs to be aware of the transitions made in the presentation of a case. Only then can he or she put the pieces together intelligently.

7. Justify the Conclusion. A sign of an inexperienced writer is a statement of conclusion that is not justified or supported by the evidence. To the writer, a conclusion may be obvious because of his or her research into the subject. The reader, however, cannot be expected to "buy" a conclusion unless all the facts supporting it are given.

1. A disorganized writer fails to _____ the ideas that are facts and those that are opinions.

2. After the facts and opinions have been presented, the reader must decide whether or not to _____ with the writer.

3. When writers are organized, they are able to lead readers and show the _____ of the discussion.

4. A writer's conclusions must be supported by the _____ .

5. For example, in paragraph 5 Washington supports his conclusion that _____ are not needed to develop the South by showing how well Southern blacks could do the job.

8 | Dusk of Dawn

W. E. B. DuBois

AUTHOR NOTES—
W. E. B. DuBois was born in Massachusetts in 1868. He was the first black person to receive a Ph.D. from Harvard University, and was one of the most important leaders of black protest in the United States. In the early 1900s DuBois was the leading opponent of racial discrimination and was respected as a historian and sociologist. He developed the concept of Pan-Africanism, the belief that all people of African descent should work together to conquer prejudice.

Believing that college-educated blacks should lead the fight against prejudice, DuBois strongly opposed educator Booker T. Washington's view that blacks could advance themselves faster through hard work than by demanding equal rights.

DuBois wrote many books and essays based on his ideas, and received a number of awards, including the Spingarn Medal in 1920. He founded the Niagra Movement in 1920 and helped found the National Association for the Advancement of Colored People (NAACP). In 1961 DuBois joined the Communist Party and moved to Ghana, living there until his death in 1963.

VOCABULARY, PART ONE—
All of these terms are in the story you are about to read. Study each term and its meaning. Then answer the questions below.

As you read the story, notice how each vocabulary term is used. You will have more questions about the terms later.

capital, money or property that makes up a person's wealth

cajoled, persuaded by the use of pleasant words; flattered

deviation, a turn in a different direction; change

undisputed, unquestioned

conceded, gave in to; accepted

discrepancies, differences; distinctions

onus, burden; obligation

unobtrusive, inconspicuous

suave, polite in a smooth, agreeable way

thwarted, kept from doing something

1. Which word tells what a mother did when she persuaded her child to eat by telling him what a good boy he was? _____

2. Which word might describe a waiter who kept smiling no matter how much you criticized the restaurant's food? _____

3. Which word could describe what a candidate did when she admitted that she had lost the election? _____

4. Which word tells what you did to your dog when you put up a fence so that he could not get out? _____

5. Which word could describe the results of a test that everyone agreed were fair and correct? _____

A READING PURPOSE —

In this selection DuBois makes clear his specific disagreements with Booker T. Washington. Read to find out what those were.

1 Since the controversy between myself and Mr. Washington has become historic, it deserves more careful statement than it has had hitherto, both as to the matters and the motives involved. There was first of all the ideological controversy. I believed in the higher education of a Talented Tenth who through their knowledge of modern culture could guide the American Negro into a higher civilization. I knew that without this the Negro would have to accept white leadership, and that such leadership could not always be trusted to guide this group into self-realization and to its highest cultural possibilities. Mr. Washington, on the other hand, believed that the Negro as an efficient worker could gain wealth and that eventually through his ownership of capital he would be able to achieve a recognized place in American culture and could then educate his children as he might wish and develop his possibilities. For this reason he proposed to put the emphasis at present upon training in the skilled trades and encouragement in industry and common labor.

2 These two theories of Negro progress were not absolutely contradictory. I recognized the importance of the Negro gaining a foothold in trades and his encouragement in industry and common labor. Mr. Washington was not absolutely opposed to college training, and sent his own children to college. But he did minimize its importance, and discouraged the philanthropic support of higher education; while I openly and repeatedly criticized what seemed to me the poor work and small accomplishment of the Negro industrial school. Moreover, it was characteristic of the Washington statesmanship that whatever he or anybody believed or wanted must be subordinated to dominant public opinion and that opinion deferred to and cajoled until it allowed a deviation toward better ways. This is no new thing in the world, but it is always dangerous.

3 But beyond this difference of ideal lay another and more bitter and insistent controversy. This started with the rise at Tuskegee Institute, and centering around Booker T. Washington, of what I may call the Tuskegee Machine. Of its existence and work, little has ever been said and almost nothing written. The years from 1899 to 1905 marked the culmination of the career of Booker T. Washington. In 1899 Mr. Washington, Paul Laurence Dunbar, and myself spoke on the same platform at the Hollis Street Theatre, Boston, before a distinguished audience. Mr. Washington was not at his best and friends immediately raised a fund which sent him to Europe for a three months' rest. He was received with extraordinary honors: he had tea with the aged Queen Victoria, but two years before her death; he was entertained by two dukes and other members of the aristocracy; he met James Bryce and Henry M.

Stanley; he was received at the Peace Conference at The Hague and was greeted by many distinguished Americans, like ex-President Harrison, Archbishop Ireland and two justices of the Supreme Court. Only a few years before he had received an honorary degree from Harvard; in 1901, he received a LL.D. from Dartmouth and that same year he dined with President Roosevelt to the consternation of the white South.

> DuBois points out the discrepancies and paradoxes in Booker T. Washington's leadership.

4 Returning to America he became during the administrations of Theodore Roosevelt and William Taft, from 1901 to 1912, the political referee in all Federal appointments or action taken with reference to the Negro and in many regarding the white South. In 1903 Andrew Carnegie made the future of Tuskegee certain by a gift of $600,000. There was no question of Booker T. Washington's underlined undisputed leadership of the ten million Negroes in America, a leadership recognized gladly by the whites and conceded by most of the Negroes.

5 But there were discrepancies and paradoxes in this leadership. It did not seem fair, for instance, that on the one hand Mr. Washington should decry political activities among Negroes, and on the other hand dictate Negro political objectives from Tuskegee. At a time when Negro civil rights called for organized and aggressive defense, he broke down that defense by advising acquiescence or at least no open agitation. During the period when laws disfranchising the Negro were being passed in all the Southern states, between 1890 and 1909, and when these were being supplemented by "Jim Crow" travel laws and other enactments making color caste legal, his public speeches, while they did not entirely ignore this development, tended continually to excuse it, to emphasize the shortcomings of the Negro, and were interpreted widely as putting the chief onus for his condition upon the Negro himself.

6 All this naturally aroused increasing opposition among Negroes and especially among the younger classes of educated Negroes, who were beginning to emerge here and there, especially from Northern institutions. This opposition began to become vocal in 1901 when two men, Monroe Trotter, Harvard 1895, and George Forbes, Amherst 1895, began the publication of the Boston *Guardian*. The *Guardian* was bitter, satirical, and personal; but it was well-edited, it was earnest, and it published facts. It attracted wide attention among colored people; it circulated among them all over the country; it was quoted and discussed. I did not wholly agree with the *Guardian,* and indeed only a few Negroes did, but nearly all read it and were influenced by it.

7 This beginning of organized opposition, together with other events, led to the growth at Tuskegee of what I have called the Tuskegee Machine. It arose first quite naturally. Not only did presidents of the United States consult Booker Washington, but governors and congressmen; philanthropists conferred with him, scholars wrote to him. Tuskegee became a vast information bureau and center of advice. It was not merely passive in these matters but, guided by a young unobtrusive minor official who was also intelligent, suave and far-seeing, active efforts were made to concentrate influence at Tuskegee. After a time almost no Negro institution could collect funds without the recommendation or acquiescence of Mr. Washington. Few political appointments were made anywhere in the United States without his consent. Even the careers of rising young colored men were very often determined by his advice and certainly his opposition was fatal. How much Mr. Washington knew of this work of the Tuskegee Machine and was directly responsible, one cannot say, but of its general activity and scope he must have been aware.

8 Moreover, it must not be forgotten that this Tuskegee Machine was not solely the idea and activity of black folk at Tuskegee. It was largely encouraged and given financial aid through certain white groups and individuals in the North. This Northern group had clear objectives. They were capitalists and employers and yet in most cases sons, relatives, or friends of the abolitionists who had sent teachers into the new Negro South after the war. These younger men believed that the Negro problem could not remain a matter of philanthropy. It must be a matter of business. These Negroes were not to be encouraged as voters in the new democracy, nor were they to be left at the mercy of the reactionary South. They were good laborers and they might be better. They could become a strong labor force and properly guided they would restrain the unbridled demands of white labor, born of the Northern labor unions and now spreading to the South.

9 One danger must be avoided and that was to allow the silly idealism of Negroes, half-trained in Southern missionary "colleges," to mislead the mass of laborers and keep them stirred-up by ambitions

incapable of realization. To this school of thought, the philosophy of Booker Washington came as a godsend and it proposed by building up his prestige and power to control the Negro group. The control was to be drastic. The Negro intelligentsia was to be suppressed and hammered into conformity. The process involved some cruelty and disappointment, but that was inevitable. This was the real force back of the Tuskegee Machine. It had money and it had opportunity, and it found in Tuskegee tools to do its bidding.

10 There were some rather pitiful results in <u>thwarted</u> ambition and curtailed opportunity. I remember one case which always stands in my memory as typical. There was a young colored man, one of the most beautiful human beings I have ever seen, with smooth brown skin, velvet eyes of intelligence, and raven hair. He was educated and well-to-do. He proposed to use his father's Alabama farm and fortune to build a Negro town and independent economic unit in the South. He furnished a part of the capital but soon needed more and he came North to get it. He struggled for more than a decade; philanthropists and capitalists were fascinated by his personality and story; and when, according to current custom, they appealed to Tuskegee for confirmation, there was silence. Mr. Washington would not say a word in favor of the project. He simply kept

still. Will Benson struggled on with ups and downs, but always balked by a whispering galley of suspicion, because his plan was never endorsed by Tuskegee. In the midst of what seemed to us who looked on the beginnings of certain success, Benson died of overwork, worry, and a broken heart.

11 From facts like this, one may gauge the bitterness of the fight of young Negroes against Mr. Washington and Tuskegee. Contrary to most opinion, the controversy as it developed was not entirely against Mr. Washington's ideas, but became the insistence upon the right of other Negroes to have and express their ideas. Things came to such a pass that when any Negro complained or advocated a course of action, he was silenced with the remark that Mr. Washington did not agree with this. Naturally the bumptious, irritated, young black intelligentsia of the day declared, "I don't care a damn what Booker Washington thinks! This is what I think, and *I have a right to think*."

Starting Time	
Reading Time	
Finishing Time	
Reading Rate	

COMPREHENSION —

Read the following questions and statements. For each one, put an X in the box before the option that contains the most complete or accurate answer.

1. Which of the following men donated a sizable amount of money to Tuskegee Institute?
   - ☐ a. John Rockefeller
   - ☐ b. Andrew Carnegie
   - ☐ c. John Paul Getty
   - ☐ d. Howard Hughes

2. DuBois wanted the Talented Tenth of his race to receive higher education because he
   - ☐ a. did not believe in mass education.
   - ☐ b. believed black aspirations could not be realized any other way.
   - ☐ c. was diametrically opposed to Booker T. Washington.
   - ☐ d. favored the establishment of a separate black state.

3. DuBois makes his point clear by
   - ☐ a. outlining Booker T. Washington's accomplishments.
   - ☐ b. contrasting his views with those of Booker T. Washington.
   - ☐ c. listing famous figures who oppose Booker T. Washington.
   - ☐ d. highlighting Booker T. Washington's subtle aggression.

4. DuBois opposed Washington's philosophy because he felt it was
   - ☐ a. a tool of the white establishment.
   - ☐ b. too militant.
   - ☐ c. built on too much ideology.
   - ☐ d. a forerunner of black militancy.

5. According to DuBois, Booker T. Washington
   - ☐ a. focused on the intellectual achievements of blacks.
   - ☐ b. favored organized and aggressive agitation.
   - ☐ c. was loud in his condemnation of inequities toward blacks.
   - ☐ d. bears some responsibility for the enactment of discriminatory laws.

6. The white establishment supported Washington because
   - ☐ a. it believed in his policies.
   - ☐ b. he was the undisputed black leader.
   - ☐ c. he was a respected member of the intelligentsia.
   - ☐ d. his policies did not threaten the status quo.

7. Which of the following best expresses Booker T. Washington's philosophy?
   - ☐ a. All things come to him who waits.
   - ☐ b. The crudest lies are often told in silence.
   - ☐ c. A bird in the hand is worth two in the bush.
   - ☐ d. Let ignorance talk as it will, learning has its value.

8. The tone of this selection is one of
   - ☐ a. undying hope.
   - ☐ b. unapologetic opposition.
   - ☐ c. hopeless apathy.
   - ☐ d. impending doom.

9. DuBois may be classified as
   - ☐ a. retiring.
   - ☐ b. regal.
   - ☐ c. disorganized.
   - ☐ d. assertive.

10. DuBois's discussion of Booker T. Washington includes elements of
    - ☐ a. folklore.
    - ☐ b. biography.
    - ☐ c. poetry.
    - ☐ d. figurative language.

Comprehension Skills

1. recalling specific facts
2. retaining concepts
3. organizing facts
4. understanding the main idea
5. drawing a conclusion
6. making a judgment
7. making an inference
8. recognizing tone
9. understanding characters
10. appreciating literary forms

VOCABULARY, PART TWO —

Write the term that makes the most sense in each sentence.

capital   undisputed
conceded   discrepancies
thwarted

1. DuBois admitted that Washington was the _____ leader of American blacks; very few people questioned his authority.

2. He realized that he and Washington had very different ideas on blacks in America and pointed out some of these _____.

3. He was honest in his presentation; however, he _____ that he and Washington did not disagree on everything.

4. Washington believed that blacks could amass _____ and thus have financial success by hard labor.

5. DuBois believed without educated leaders to guide them, blacks would be _____ from achieving success.

onus   unobtrusive
suave   cajoled
deviation

6. A young black man that DuBois knew took upon himself the _____ of raising money for a business.

7. He was not a(n) _____, smooth talker who could charm people into helping him.

8. He used _____ methods like quietly presenting his case to men in business.

9. Washington could have _____ important people into helping the young man by using his own charm and influence.

10. However, Washington would have seen this as a

_____ from what he believed

in and was unwilling to change in this way.

Comprehension Score [ ]

Vocabulary Score [ ]

W R I T I N G —

What would DuBois and Washington say to each other if they met? Pretend you have been at a meeting at which both men explained their ideas. Write a few paragraphs that summarize what each might have said. Use material from this and the preceding selection to support your ideas.

S T U D Y   S K I L L S —

Read the following passage and answer the questions that follow it.

How to Use Word Context

During political campaigns in election years, we invariably hear one candidate accuse an opponent of quoting him "out of context." The danger in taking a speaker's words out of context is that a sentence by itself may suggest a meaning entirely different from the meaning it conveyed when surrounded by other thoughts.

This suggests an important principle of word usage: a word's true meaning depends upon how it is used. This is readily apparent in the case of ambiguous words, like *bow* or *sink*. Context tells the reader when a *bow tied with ribbon* is meant rather than a *bow to the audience*. Similarly, without knowing the context the reader does not know whether the writer is referring to *sink* as in *go down in the water* or *sink* as in *kitchen*.

Not so apparent is the effect of context on words generally thought to have a consistent and unchanging meaning. The word *conventional* in one context may suggest all that is stable, reliable, and in the most time-honored tradition. In another context *conventional* could

imply staleness, the refusal to change or adapt to modern ways.

Beginning as youngsters, we add to our understanding of a word's meaning every time we hear it or use it. For example, the first few times you heard the word *school*, you may have understood it to mean a place where older brothers and sisters spend most of the day. Later, *school* came to mean a place where things are learned. Today, your understanding of the word encompasses several additional ideas.

This same growth pattern occurs with other words. As a student, you will come across new words, or words you only vaguely understand. Being aware of the way words function in context helps you to understand these words and make them part of your vocabulary. Each time you hear an unfamiliar word, the context it is being used in will add to your understanding. With repeated exposure, you will come to understand all that the word implies, and eventually you will be able to use it comfortably in your writing and speaking.

1. Quoting a speaker's words out of context may result in conveying a _____ meaning from the one intended.

2. Some words are _____ and change meaning completely when used in different contexts.

3. DuBois, for instance, uses the word *capital* to mean "money," but it could also refer to the city in each _____ where the governor and the legislature pass laws.

3. Context may also have an unexpected _____ on words generally thought to have unchanging meanings.

5. Complete understanding of a word results in the ability to use it correctly in _____ and in speaking.

9 Sweet Lorraine

James Baldwin

AUTHOR NOTES—
Novelist and essayist James Baldwin was born in 1924 in New York City. The first of nine children, he grew up in Harlem, where his father was a minister. When he was 24, Baldwin left the United States for a ten-year stay in Europe. Residing mainly in Paris, he wrote and published his first three books. In 1957 Baldwin returned to the United States to join the civil rights struggle. For the next several years he divided his time between a home in Southern France and one in New York City. He then returned to Europe permanently, where he died in 1987.

Baldwin's published works include, among others, his semiautobiographical first novel, *Go Tell It on the Mountain*, as well as *Another Country*, a novel examining racial and sexual issues, and the essay collection *Notes of a Native Son*. He also achieved recognition for two plays, *Blues for Mister Charlie* and *The Amen Corner*. His stories and essays have appeared in many magazines and essays both here and abroad.

VOCABULARY, PART ONE—
All of these terms are in the story you are about to read. Study each term and its meaning. Then answer the questions below.

As you read the story, notice how each vocabulary term is used. You will have more questions about the terms later.

constricted, tightened up to stop the natural course of development

corroborated, strengthened or assured

incessantly, unceasingly; constantly

astringent, bitter

wry, drily humorous; ironic

assuage, soothe; ease

suffused, spread over or spread through

banal, commonplace; uninteresting

insurgent, person who revolts; rebel

holocaust, widescale destruction of a whole group of people, by fire or other means

1. Which word tells what ointments do that you rub on burns to get rid of the pain?

   _____

2. Which word could describe the humor of a person who often makes fun of himself?

   _____

3. Which word could be an antonym for *sweet*? _____

4. Which word tells what an ink stain did when it spread over a large section of a

   shirt? _____

5. Which word could be a synonym for *boring*? _____

A R E A D I N G P U R P O S E —

In this selection Baldwin remembers Lorraine Hansberry, the talented playwright who wrote *A Raisin in the Sun*. Read to find out his feelings about her and her work.

1 That's the way I always felt about her, and so I won't apologize for calling her that now. *She* understood it: in that far too brief a time when we walked and talked and laughed and drank together, sometimes in the streets and bars and restaurants of the Village, sometimes at her house, sometimes at my house, sometimes gracelessly fleeing the houses of others; and sometimes seeming, for anyone who didn't know us, to be having a knockdown drag-out battle. We spent a lot of time arguing about history and tremendously related subjects in her Bleecker Street and, later, Waverly Place flat. And often, just when I was certain that she was about to throw me out, as being altogether too rowdy a type, she would stand up, her hands on her hips (for these down-home sessions she always wore slacks) and pick up my empty glass as though she intended to throw it at me. Then she would walk into the kitchen, saying, with a haughty toss of her head, "Really, Jimmy. You ain't *right*, child!" With which stern put-down, she would hand me another drink and launch into a brilliant analysis of just why I wasn't "right." I would often stagger down her stairs as the sun came up, usually in the middle of a paragraph and always in the middle of a laugh. That marvelous laugh. That marvelous face. I loved her, she was my sister and my comrade. Her going did not so much make me lonely as make me realize how lonely we were. We had that respect for each other which perhaps is only felt by people on the same side of the barricades, listening to the accumulating thunder of the hooves of horses and the treads of tanks.

2 The first time I ever saw Lorraine was at the Actors' Studio, in the winter of '57–58. She was there as an observer of the Workshop Production of *Giovanni's Room*. She sat way up in the bleachers, taking on some of the biggest names in the American theater because she had liked the play and they, in the main, hadn't. I was enormously grateful to her, she seemed to speak for me; and afterwards she talked to me with a gentleness and generosity never to be forgotten. A small, shy, determined person, with that strength dictated by absolutely impersonal ambition: she was not trying to "make it"—she was trying to keep the faith.

3 We really met, however, in Philadelphia, in 1959, when *A Raisin in the Sun* was at the beginning of its amazing career. Much has been written about this play; I personally feel that it will demand a far less guilty and <u>constricted</u> people than the present-day Americans to be able to assess it at all; as an historical achievement, anyway, no one can gainsay its importance. What is relevant here is that I had never in my life seen so many black people in the theater. And the reason was that never before, in the entire history of the American theater, had so much of the truth of black people's lives been seen on the stage. Black people ignored the theater because the theater had always ignored them.

4   But, in *Raisin,* black people recognized that house and all the people in it—the mother, the son, the daughter and the daughter-in-law, and supplied the play with an interpretative element which could not be present in the minds of white people: a kind of claustrophobic terror, created not only by their knowledge of the house but by their knowledge of the streets. And when the curtain came down, Lorraine and I found ourselves in the backstage alley, where she was immediately mobbed. I produced a pen and Lorraine handed me her handbag and began signing autographs. "It only happens once," she said. I stood there and watched. I watched the people, who loved Lorraine for what she had brought to them; and watched Lorraine, who loved the people for what they brought to *her.* It was not, for her, a matter of being admired. She was being corroborated and confirmed. She was wise enough and honest enough to recognize that black American artists are a very special case. One is not merely an artist and one is not judged merely as an artist: the black people crowding around Lorraine, whether or not they considered her an artist, assuredly considered her a witness. This country's concept of art and artists has the effect, scarcely worth mentioning by now, of isolating the artist from the people. One can see the effect of this in the irrelevance of so much of the work produced by celebrated white artists; but the effect of this isolation on a black artist is absolutely fatal. He *is,* already, as a black American citizen, isolated from most of his white countrymen. At the crucial hour, he can hardly look to his artistic peers for help, for they do not know enough about him to be able to correct him. To continue to grow, to remain in touch with himself, he needs the support of that community from which, however, all of the pressures of American life incessantly conspire to remove him. And when he is effectively removed, he falls silent—and the people have lost another hope.

5   Much of the strain under which Lorraine worked was produced by her knowledge of this reality, and her determined refusal to be destroyed by it. She was a very young woman, with an overpowering vision, and fame had come to her early—she must certainly have wished, often enough, that fame had seen fit to drag its feet a little. For fame and recognition are not synonyms, especially not here, and her fame was to cause her to be criticized very harshly, very loudly, and very often by both black and white people who were unable to believe, apparently, that a really serious intention could be contained in so

> What happens to a
> dream deferred?
> Does it dry up like a
> raisin in the sun?...
> —Langston Hughes

glamorous a frame. She took it all with a kind of astringent good humor, refusing, for example, even to consider defending herself when she was being accused of being a "slum-lord" because of her family's real-estate holdings in Chicago. I called her during that time, and all she said—with a wry laugh—was, "My God, Jimmy, do you realize you're only the second person who's called me today? And you know how my phone kept ringing *before!*" She was not surprised. She was devoted to the human race, but she was not romantic about it.

6   When so bright a light goes out so early, when so gifted an artist goes so soon, we are left with a sorrow and wonder which speculation cannot assuage. One is filled for a long time with a sense of injustice as futile as it is powerful. And the vanished person fills the mind, in this or that attitude, doing this or that. Sometimes, very briefly, one hears the exact inflection of the voice, the exact timbre of the laugh—as I have, when watching the dramatic presentation, *To Be Young, Gifted and Black,* and in reading through these pages. But I do not have the heart to presume to assess her work, for all of it, for me, was suffused with the light which was Lorraine. It is possible, for example, that *The Sign in Sidney Brustein's Window* attempts to say too much; but it is also exceedingly probable that it makes so loud and uncomfortable a sound because of the surrounding silence; not many plays, presently, risk being accused of attempting to say too much! Again, Brustein is certainly a very *willed* play, unabashedly didactic; but it cannot, finally, be dismissed or categorized in this way because of the astonishing life of its people. It positively courts being dismissed as old-fashioned and banal and yet has the unmistakable power of turning the viewer's judgment in on himself. *Is all this true or not true?* the play rudely demands; and, unforgivably, leaves us squirming before this question. One cannot quite answer the question negatively, one risks being caught in a lie. But an affirmative answer imposes a new level of responsibility, both for one's conduct and for the fortunes of the American state, and one risks, therefore, the disagreeable necessity of becoming "an insurgent again." For Lorraine made no bones about asserting that art has a purpose, and that its purpose was

action: that it contained the "energy which could change things."

[7] It would be good, selfishly, to have her around now, that small, dark girl, with her wit, her wonder, and her eloquent compassion. I've only met one person Lorraine couldn't get through to, and that was the late Bobby Kennedy. And, as the years have passed since that stormy meeting (Lorraine talks about it in these pages, so I won't go into it here) I've very often pondered what she then tried to convey—that a <u>holocaust</u> is no respector of persons; that what, today, seems merely humiliation and injustice for a few, can, unchecked, become Terror for the many, snuffing out white lives just as though they were black lives; that if the American state could not protect the lives of black citizens, then, presently, the entire State would find itself engulfed. And the horses and tanks are indeed upon us, and the end is not in sight. Perhaps it is just as well, after all, that she did not live to see with the outward eye what she saw so clearly with the inward one. And it is not at all farfetched to suspect that what she saw contributed to the strain which killed her, for the effort to which Lorraine was dedicated is more than enough to kill a man. ■

[8] I saw Lorraine in her hospital bed, as she was dying. She tried to speak, she couldn't. She did not seem frightened or sad, only exasperated that her body no longer obeyed her; she smiled and waved. But I prefer to remember her as she was the last time I saw her on her feet. We were at, of all places, the PEN Club, she was seated, talking, dressed all in black, wearing a very handsome wide, black hat, thin, and radiant. I knew she had been ill, but I didn't know, then, how seriously. I said, "Lorraine, baby, you look beautiful, how in the world do you do it?" She was leaving, I have the impression she was on a staircase, and she turned and smiled that smile and said, "It helps to develop a serious illness, Jimmy!" and waved and disappeared.

Starting Time   [   ]

Reading Time   [   ]

Finishing Time   [   ]

Reading Rate   [   ]

COMPREHENSION —

Read the following questions and statements. For each one, put an X in the box before the option that contains the most complete or accurate answer.

1. The first time the author saw Lorraine Hansberry was at the Actors' Studio where she was observing the production of
   - ☐ a. *A Raisin in the Sun.*
   - ☐ b. *To Be Young, Gifted and Black.*
   - ☐ c. *The Sign in Sidney Brustein's Window.*
   - ☐ d. *Giovanni's Room.*

2. The author of this article
   - ☐ a. tolerated Lorraine.
   - ☐ b. admired Lorraine.
   - ☐ c. despised Lorraine.
   - ☐ d. pitied Lorraine.

3. The writer presents details according to
   - ☐ a. a rough time order.
   - ☐ b. order of importance.
   - ☐ c. spatial order.
   - ☐ d. cause and effect.

4. Choose the best title for this selection.
   - ☐ a. Black and Successful
   - ☐ b. The Light of Blackness
   - ☐ c. Gone but Not Forgotten
   - ☐ d. A Great Defense

5. This passage hints that
   - ☐ a. few plays are written for a black audience.
   - ☐ b. black slumlords are well respected.
   - ☐ c. fame and recognition often ruin a person.
   - ☐ d. America is a land of opportunity.

6. We can make the judgment that Hansberry's play *The Sign in Sidney Brustein's Window* is
   - ☐ a. sarcastic.
   - ☐ b. thought-provoking.
   - ☐ c. enjoyably humorous.
   - ☐ d. grossly entertaining.

7. In order for a black artist to succeed, he or she
   - ☐ a. has to learn how to take positive criticism.
   - ☐ b. cannot be involved with militant blacks.
   - ☐ c. should be aware of black power.
   - ☐ d. must not be isolated from American society.

8. From the tone of this selection, we can see that the writer
   - ☐ a. has a great sense of humor.
   - ☐ b. possesses a violent temper.
   - ☐ c. is filled with a sense of loss.
   - ☐ d. builds a suspenseful story.

9. Hansberry seems to have been
   - ☐ a. an independent person.
   - ☐ b. an angry person.
   - ☐ c. a shy person.
   - ☐ d. a generous person.

10. The last sentence of the passage shows the use of
    - ☐ a. alliteration.
    - ☐ b. description.
    - ☐ c. personification.
    - ☐ d. sarcasm.

Comprehension Skills

1. recalling specific facts
2. retaining concepts
3. organizing facts
4. understanding the main idea
5. drawing a conclusion
6. making a judgment
7. making an inference
8. recognizing tone
9. understanding characters
10. appreciating literary forms

VOCABULARY, PART TWO—

Write the term that makes the most sense in each sentence.

incessantly   astringent
wry   banal
insurgent

1. Some of the arguments Baldwin had with Hansberry were exciting and interesting; others were

   _____.

2. She was not a person who talked

   _____, nor was she unusually quiet.

3. She had a(n) _____ outlook that saw the humor even in some difficult situations.

4. In some ways she was a(n)

   _____, a rebel.

5. Recognizing that she was dying was like taking a very _____ medicine.

constricted   corroborated
suffused   holocaust
assuage

6. Though he tried various remedies, it was hard for Baldwin to _____ his grief after her death.

7. The pain _____ his body, and he could feel it in every pore of his skin.

8. His throat _____, and he had difficulty breathing.

9. His and Hansberry's friends _____ his pain; they too were suffering from her death.

10. Only when he thought of a _____ destroying vast numbers of people did he realize that there could be much worse pain than his.

Comprehension Score   ☐

Vocabulary Score   ☐

WRITING —

Even though they sometimes disagreed, Baldwin and Lorraine Hansberry supported each other through difficult times. Do you have a friend with whom you have a similar relationship (or do you know of such a friendship among two other people)? Write a few paragraphs about the friendship, using specific examples to point out why it is special.

STUDY SKILLS —

Read the following passage and answer the questions that follow it.

Contextual Aids, I

Context helps us in a way no dictionary can. Various shades and richness of meaning cannot be gained from dictionary definitions alone; we must see the word used to grasp its full meaning.

Studies of good readers show that they are aware of the different contexts in which words are set. These are sometimes referred to as contextual aids. Using contextual aids intelligently is the reader's most important vocabulary tool. And it is a reading skill that can be mastered and developed.

1. Common Expressions. Certain common phrases and idiomatic expressions are used regularly and become well known to the reader. In a familiar saying like *His bark is worse than his* _____ , the reader can easily fill in the missing word, *bite*. If you came across a similar expression in your reading, you could automatically supply any missing elements because of the phrase's familiarity.

2. Modifying Phrases. Frequently a word is accompanied by a modifying phrase that gives the reader valuable clues to understanding and recognition. For example, if you were to read the sentence _____ *by the finest artists of our century were displayed at the exhibit,* you could easily figure out that the missing word is *Paintings*. The phrase *by the finest artists* is the contextual aid that acts as the clue.

1. Using contextual aids is an important reading

   _____ .

2. Words that are part of a _____

   phrase are easily recognized.

3. The word omitted can be supplied because of its

   _____ .

4. Baldwin uses such an expression when he writes in

   paragraph 1 of a "knockdown, _____

   battle."

5. Unknown words can sometimes be understood

   through the use of accompanying phrases that

   _____ the words.

10 The Hottest Water in Chicago

Gayle Pemberton

AUTHOR NOTES—
Gayle Pemberton was born in St. Paul, Minnesota, in 1948. She has an undergraduate degree in English from the University of Michigan and a Ph.D from Harvard in English and American literature. Currently the director of African American studies at Princeton University, Pemberton has also taught at, among others, Smith College, Columbia University, and Northwestern University.

VOCABULARY, PART ONE—
All of these terms are in the story you are about to read. Study each term and its meaning. Then answer the questions below.

As you read the story, notice how each vocabulary term is used. You will have more questions about the terms later.

dowdy, shabby; unfashionable

artery, a main or important road

minuscule, very small

ambled, strolled

intact, in one piece

proprietor, owner

alleviate, relieve; lessen

assented, agreed

desolation, ruined, bare, or empty condition

verify, prove the accuracy of

1. Which term could describe the condition of a vase that fell to the floor but didn't break? _____

2. Which term tells how someone walked? _____

3. Which term could describe the appearance of a young woman who dressed as if she were 70 years old? _____

4. Which term could you use if you were saying you only wanted a tiny piece of something? _____

5. Which term describes the effect that something like aspirin can have on pain?

    _____

A READING PURPOSE —

This selection describes an incident that the narrator was involved in not long after her mother was stabbed. As you read, try to form an opinion of the kind of person the narrator is.

---

¹ One Chicago morning, I gathered up a pair of my trustiest work shoes—a pair that a student of mine once said made me look schoolmarmish and <u>dowdy</u>, to which I replied, "So find me some that are *au courant*, reasonable, and won't cripple me"—noticed their failing heels and went directly to a shoe repair shop. I had been clearing the last of my things out of my sister's apartment in anticipation of Mother's arrival. After she had been stabbed in her home we had spent weeks sorting out the effects of three generations' worth of living, finding minor treasures of letters, photographs, and books belonging to my grandparents, my parents, my sister, and me. My sister was in Kansas City for the final leg, helping Mother with the paperwork to sell the house, engaging the movers.

² The gray was bright, the sun poked through clouds, an early spring snowstorm was being rapidly thawed by late spring temperatures. I decided to walk, to think about the move and hope that Mother would withstand the aftershocks as well as she had the major earthquake that had so brutally changed the course of her life. I also wanted to try to get some of the sand and rock-salt and fear out of my body and brain, to move my joints freely again. I was on my way to Jeffery Boulevard, a relatively short <u>artery</u> that cuts off Lake Shore Drive,

■ about twenty blocks south of the Museum of Science and Industry, the University of Chicago, and Hyde Park.

³ Jeffery Boulevard is a main drag of South Shore, lined with the kinds of businesses that define black communities throughout the country. I walked along Seventy-first Street to get there. I passed empty storefronts with gated doorways—the modern portcullis effect—with rusting metal, Master and Yale locks still in place, piles of mud, newspapers, torn lottery tickets, half-pints of Old Blind Boy, and dog manure holding tight against the woven metal. Urban tumbleweed. There was a <u>minuscule</u> automobile body shop; a bakery still in business; a couple of gutted buildings; small grocery stores advertising soda, cigarettes, liquor, and potato chips, one or two run by Middle Easterners, some by blacks, some too filthy to enter. Groups of men stood talking to each other outside of the stores, as little children scampered in with greenbacks crumpled in their hands, often accompanied by handwritten notes, buying a candy bar, two packs of Kools, a loaf of bread, and a gallon of milk. I <u>ambled</u> past the half-dozen liquor stores that I recall seeing closed only in the wee hours of the morning; a currency exchange, where for a percentage of the total a paycheck can be cashed, money orders

bought, telephone bills paid; a dry cleaners; the remnants of three failed restaurants at one site; a fish house; an Armed Forces recruiting station; a drugstore; and a few clothing and shoe stores hanging on in the face of the lower overhead and lower prices the large Loop chains could offer.

> Walking down the city streets, this narrator discovers, could have a definite effect on one's mood. But was her harsh reaction justified?

4   It seemed I saw only men and boys that morning, boys from about five years of age through preadolescence in various stages of outrage at each other, some fighting, some grumbling; teenagers gesturing at each other threateningly, or laughing, or snarling, tugging at their genitals every few minutes or so, making sure their manhood was <u>intact</u>. Quite a few of the little boys, teenagers, and men wore plastic bags on their heads—clear or opaque shower caps they seemed, in the chemical-setting stage of the latter-day conk called a curl or jericurl. The older men used their hands only to highlight their speech. A few of them had bloodshot eyes; they wore old shoes and clothes, dingy stingy brims, lusterless pinkie rings.

5   I reached Jeffery Boulevard just as the sun broke free, making my neck hot as I crossed the threshold of the shoe repair shop.

6   It was a standard shoe shop: smells of polish and machine oil, piles of bagged and unbagged shoes tagged behind the counter, a few posters advertising dances and cabarets, an outdated calendar from a local church, cans of Kiwi and Esquire, bottles of Shinola, some dusty packages of shoestrings, a deposit-for-work-necessary sign. Under the glass counter, a couple of handmade purses—consignment sales—and some used, but repaired and shined out-of-style pumps and sling-backs for sale.

7   Three men were in the shop; one, the <u>proprietor</u>, had on a work apron, the other two sat on stools in coats. They didn't stop their conversation as I entered, nor did they look my way. The proprietor was making a serious point:

8   "I say it's the truth. The Bible don't lie. If it's in the Bible then it's true."

9   "Yeah," said the first man, nodding his head.

10   "Isn't that the truth?" said the second.

11   "Genesis is true. The Lord God made the world in six days and rested on the seventh," preached the proprietor.

12   "Lawd, that's true," said the first man.

13   "Uh-huh," from the second.

14   "And Noah put animals, two by two, on the Ark, and everything else died in the flood," opined the proprietor.

15   "Ain't that the truth."

16   "Yes."

17   "And God created Eve from the rib of Adam," he slapped his left hand into his right palm.

18   "That's sure 'nuff true."

19   "That's what it says, the Bible is true."

20   I bounced from one foot to another, my old dowdies resting on the counter. I looked at the men. They all seemed able-bodied, in a middle-middle age. I was getting angry, but I bit my tongue before I could snarl something about Eve coming before the Ark. I unzipped my jacket to <u>alleviate</u> the heat, and only after about four more minutes, bringing to an end what seemed my eternity of waiting, did the proprietor allow himself to recognize the existence of trade. He kept talking about Genesis, walked behind the counter as the other men nodded and verbally <u>assented</u> to his words. He asked me what I wanted, took out a piece of chalk and put two *X*'s on the heels, tore off a ticket, took my two-dollar deposit, and resumed his place in the trinity of holy men.

21   I walked out of the shop, getting bumped to the side by three young teenagers, two with plastic bags on their heads, who were running in and out among pedestrians, yelling obscenities. I was sorry I'd walked. I took my now stiff legs on an alternate route back, via residential streets, where I looked at houses and remembered my childhood. I have never been able to afford a house and the only one I knew intimately, which had been the scene of family triumphs and recent disaster, was being sold that weekend.

22   I was angry with the men in the shoe shop, not because I wanted them to stop their ritual or to leave their temple of shoe shop or barber shop and the rites they had reserved for themselves there. But just outside the door was <u>desolation</u> and death, and somehow the everlasting quest to <u>verify</u> the physical origins of earth was, to me, a greater blasphemy than my uncharitable thoughts. I wanted them to act in the face of all the ironies of black American life, to leave Genesis and the *fait accompli* of the

Earth's formation behind, to stop preaching to the converted and get out in the streets to do some small thing, like suggesting to young men that obsession with one's genitals stunts one's growth and that curls, though no doubt pleasing to their wearers, look like conked, greasy Afros to a whole lot of people—potential employers, for instance.

Starting Time	
Reading Time	
Finishing Time	
■ Reading Rate	

COMPREHENSION —

Read the following questions and statements. For each one, put an X in the box before the option that contains the most complete or accurate answer.

1. The purpose of the narrator's walk in this story is
   - ☐ a. to check out the condition of the neighborhood.
   - ☐ b. to report to the police what had happened to her mother.
   - ☐ c. to get her shoes repaired.
   - ☐ d. to see if spring had finally arrived.

2. By the end of the story the narrator
   - ☐ a. has vowed never to walk this route again.
   - ☐ b. recognizes she has reacted uncharitably but feels justified.
   - ☐ c. has decided to move out of the neighborhood.
   - ☐ d. feels that she made a mistake not telling the men off.

3. The time period covered in the story is approximately
   - ☐ a. forty-five minutes.
   - ☐ b. three hours.
   - ☐ c. an entire morning.
   - ☐ d. an entire day.

4. A saying that reflects the author's point of view is
   - ☐ a. All things come to him who waits.
   - ☐ b. A man's home is his castle.
   - ☐ c. Don't just stand there; do something!
   - ☐ d. People in glass houses shouldn't throw stones.

5. The narrator specifically describes sights along the street in order to
   - ☐ a. criticize the South Side of Chicago.
   - ☐ b. show that this is a run-down neighborhood.
   - ☐ c. compare this neighborhood with the place where her mother lived.
   - ☐ d. make a strong case for the need for urban renewal.

6. Talking about Adam and Eve and the Bible is, for the men in the store,
   - ☐ a. a way of being religious.
   - ☐ b. a justification for ignoring the customer.
   - ☐ c. a way of passing the time.
   - ☐ d. a way of showing their concern for other people.

7. The narrator mentions her mother's stabbing and need to move in order to
   - ☐ a. win the reader's sympathy.
   - ☐ b. explain her annoyance and impatience with what she experiences in the neighborhood.
   - ☐ c. suggest that one of the boys on the street may have been responsible.
   - ☐ d. establish a sad tone to carry throughout the story.

8. The tone created in paragraph 2 of the story is one of
   - ☐ a. deep anger.
   - ☐ b. slight annoyance.
   - ☐ c. great sadness.
   - ☐ d. cautious optimism.

9. The proprietor of the store can be characterized as
   - ☐ a. devoted to his work.
   - ☐ b. totally unconcerned about his work.
   - ☐ c. somewhat unconcerned about his work.
   - ☐ d. barely having enough work to keep his business going.

10. When the narrator speaks of "the aftershocks as well as...the major earthquake that had so brutally changed the course of her [mother's] life," she is using
□ a. personification.
□ b. a simile.
□ c. a metaphor.
□ d. alliteration.

Comprehension Skills
1. recalling specific facts
2. retaining concepts
3. organizing facts
4. understanding the main idea
5. drawing a conclusion
6. making a judgment
7. making an inference
8. recognizing tone
9. understanding characters
10. appreciating literary forms

VOCABULARY, PART TWO—
Write the term that makes the most sense in each sentence.

dowdy   artery
minuscule   ambled
alleviate

1. The narrator walked down a city _____ that connected two smaller streets.

2. She was hoping to distract her mind and thus _____ her pain over her mother's recent stabbing.

3. She _____ along rather slowly, looking at the various stores and buildings as she walked.

4. The shoes she was having repaired were plain and _____, but she didn't care what they looked like because they were comfortable.

5. The repair they needed was very minor, so she hoped the price would be _____ too.

intact   proprietor
assented   desolation
verify

6. The _____ of the repair store owned one of the few businesses still open on the street.

7. All around him were empty lots, closed businesses, and other signs of _____.

8. Many windows in the buildings were broken; only a few were _____.

9. The man gave the narrator a receipt to _____ that she had left the shoes in his store.

10. When the man told the others in the store his views about the Bible, they all nodded their heads and _____.

Comprehension Score [   ]

Vocabulary Score [   ]

WRITING—
To what extent, if any, do you think the narrator was justified in reacting as she did? Write a few paragraphs expressing your views. Use evidence from the story and from your own personal experience to back up what you say.

STUDY SKILLS—
Read the following passage and answer the questions that follow it.

Contextual Aids, II
3. Accompanying Description. An unknown word can often be understood because it has been defined or

described in the context. This kind of contextual aid, naturally enough, is commonly used in textbooks. Authors frequently provide a description or definition to assist their readers. In the sentence *Students should use _____ ; these are books containing definitions of words,* the reader would know that the missing word is *dictionaries* because of the accompanying description.

4. Parts of a Series. When items appear in a list or series, the items themselves often give clues to the reader. It one of them were omitted from the list, the reader could probably supply it. This is possible because the parts of a series are related; they share some feature in common. An additional clue is provided by the connector *and;* this tells the reader that the items are alike in some way. For example, if you see the sentence *The theater was packed with men, women, and _____,* you can confidently fill in the blank with the missing word *children,* the next word in the series. Notice how the *and* in the series leads you to expect another related item.

5. Comparison and Contrast. Unknown or unfamiliar words become meaningful when compared or contrasted with known words. We know that when parallels are being drawn, like things are being examined. In the case of contrast, we are dealing with things that are opposite. Readers' ability to recognize that a comparison or con-

trast is being made permits them to exploit this type of contextual aid. Take this sentence: *The two brothers were as different as day and _____.* It is simple for readers to complete the comparison with the word *night.*

1. The definition of words as a contextual aid is often used in _____.

2. Items in a series usually _____ some feature in common.

3. The connector word *and* indicates that the items are _____ in some way.

4. When Pemberton talks in paragraph 22 about *desolation and death,* the connector *and* helps make it clear that *desolation* has a _____ rather than a positive meaning.

5. In using the contextual aid of contrast, we are dealing with things that are _____.

Women, Race, and Class

11

Angela Y. Davis

AUTHOR NOTES—
Angela Davis, a scholar, lecturer, writer, and activist for human rights, was born in Birmingham, Alabama, in 1944. Throughout her life she has been active in struggles for democratic rights, prison and judicial reform, and student rights. Joining the Communist Party in 1968, Davis came to national attention in 1970 when she was placed on the Ten Most Wanted List and was the subject of an intense FBI hunt, leading to one of the most famous trials in United States history. Davis was acquitted after massive national and international protests.

Davis is the author of numerous essays on black liberation, political prisoners and the penal-judicial system, and the struggle for women's equality. She has published several books, including her best-selling *Angela Davis: An Autobiography*. Davis is now a professor of history of consciousness at the University of California at Santa Cruz.

VOCABULARY, PART ONE—
All of these terms are in the story you are about to read. Study each term and its meaning. Then answer the questions below.

As you read the story, notice how each vocabulary term is used. You will have more questions about the terms later.

unquantifiable, not measurable

liquidate, to do away with; settle, as a debt

arduously, in a difficult or laborious manner

accessibility, quality of being easy to use or get to

anathema, something that is strongly hated or detested

obsolescence, state of being out of date

complementary, providing the missing elements to make something complete

hierarchical, involving a group or organization in which some people are ranked over others

enigmatically, mysteriously

agrarian, relating to the land; as in farming

63

1. Which word could identify the quality of a record player that you've now replaced with a CD player? _____

2. Which word identifies what ramps leading up to buildings give to wheelchair users?

   _____

3. Which word describes how a person works who scrubs floors for eight hours a day?

   _____

4. Which word could describe an organization that has a president, senior vice presidents, junior vice presidents, senior members, and associate members?

   _____

5. Which word could describe the activities of people who work on a farm?

   _____

A READING PURPOSE—

In this selection Davis analyzes housework from both a historical and a political viewpoint. Read to learn how this work has been regarded by different peoples in different time periods.

1 The countless chores collectively known as "housework"—cooking, washing dishes, doing laundry, making beds, sweeping, shopping, etc.—apparently consume some three to four thousand hours of the average housewife's year.[1] As startling as this statistic may be, it does not even account for the constant and <u>unquantifiable</u> attention mothers must give to their children. Just as a woman's maternal duties are always taken for granted, her never-ending toil as a housewife rarely occasions expressions of appreciation within her family. Housework, after all, is virtually invisible: "No one notices it until it isn't done—we notice the unmade bed, not the scrubbed and polished floor."[2] Invisible, repetitive, exhausting, unproductive, uncreative—these are the adjectives which most perfectly capture the nature of housework.

2 The new consciousness associated with the contemporary women's movement has encouraged increasing numbers of women to demand that their men provide some relief from this drudgery. Already, more men have begun to assist their partners around the house, some of them even devoting equal time to household chores. But how many of these men have liberated themselves from the assumption that housework is "women's work"? How many of them would not characterize their house-cleaning activities as "helping" their women partners?

3 If it were at all possible simultaneously to <u>liquidate</u> the idea that housework is women's work and to redistribute it equally to men and women alike, would this constitute a satisfactory solution? Freed from its exclusive affiliation with the female sex, would housework thereby cease to be oppressive? While most women would joyously hail the advent of the "househusband," the desexualization of domestic labor would not really alter the oppressive nature of the work itself. In the final analysis, neither women nor men should waste precious hours of their lives on work that is neither stimulating, creative nor productive.

4 One of the most closely guarded secrets of advanced capitalist societies involves the possibility—the real possibility—of radically transforming the nature of housework. A substantial portion of the housewife's domestic tasks can actually be incorporated into the industrial economy. In other words, housework need no longer be considered necessarily and unalterably private in character. Teams of trained and well-paid workers, moving from dwelling to dwelling, engineering technologically advanced cleaning machinery, could swiftly and efficiently accomplish what the present-day housewife does so <u>arduously</u> and

primitively. Why the shroud of silence surrounding this potential of radically redefining the nature of domestic labor? Because the capitalist economy is structurally hostile to the industrialization of housework. Socialized housework implies large government subsidies in order to guarantee <u>accessibility</u> to the working-class families whose need for such services is most obvious. Since little in the way of profits would result, industrialized housework—like all unprofitable enterprises—is <u>anathema</u> to the capitalist economy. Nonetheless, the rapid expansion of the female labor force means that more and more women are finding it increasingly difficult to excel as housewives according to the traditional standards. In other words, the industrialization of housework, along with the socialization of housework, is becoming an objective social need. Housework as individual women's private responsibility and as female labor performed under primitive technical conditions, may finally be approaching historical <u>obsolescence</u>.

5 Although housework as we know it today may eventually become a bygone relic of history, prevailing social attitudes continue to associate the eternal female condition with images of brooms and dustpans, mops and pails, aprons and stoves, pots and pans. And it is true that women's work, from one historical era to another, has been associated in general with the homestead. Yet female domestic labor has not always been what it is today, for like all social phenomena, housework is a fluid product of human history. As economic systems have arisen and faded away, the scope and quality of housework have undergone radical transformations.

6 As Frederick Engels argued in his classic work on the *Origin of the Family, Private Property and the State,*[3] sexual inequality as we know it today did not exist before the advent of private property. During early eras of human history the sexual division of labor within the system of economic production was <u>complementary</u> as opposed to <u>hierarchical</u>. In societies where men may have been responsible for hunting wild animals and women, in turn, for gathering wild vegetables and fruits, both sexes performed economic tasks that were equally essential to their community's survival. Because the community, during those eras, was essentially an extended family, women's central role in domestic affairs meant that they were accordingly valued and respected as productive members of the community.

7 The centrality of women's domestic tasks in pre-

> As the social structure undergoes change, some tasks regarded as traditional and fixed will be modified.

capitalist cultures was dramatized by a personal experience during a jeep trip I took in 1973 across the Masai Plains. On an isolated dirt road in Tanzania, I noticed six Masai women <u>enigmatically</u> balancing an enormous board on their heads. As my Tanzanian friends explained, these women were probably transporting a house roof to a new village which they were in the process of constructing. Among the Masai, as I learned, women are responsible for all domestic activities, thus also for the construction of their nomadic people's frequently relocated houses. Housework, as far as Masai women are concerned, entails not only cooking, cleaning, child-rearing, sewing, etc., but house-building as well. As important as their men's cattle-raising duties may be, the women's "housework" is no less productive and no less essential than the economic contributions of Masai men.

8 Within the pre-capitalist, nomadic economy of the Masai, women's domestic labor is as essential to the economy as the cattle-raising jobs performed by their men. As producers, they enjoy a correspondingly important social status. In advanced capitalist societies, on the other hand, the service-oriented domestic labor of housewives, who can seldom produce tangible evidence of their work, diminishes the social status of women in general. When all is said and done, the housewife, according to bourgeois ideology, is, quite simply, her husband's lifelong servant.

9 The source of the bourgeois notion of woman as man's eternal servant is itself a revealing story. Within the relatively short history of the United States, the "housewife" as a finished historical product is just a little more than a century old. Housework, during the colonial era, was entirely different from the daily work routine of the housewife in the United States today.

A woman's work began at sunup and continued by firelight as long as she could hold her eyes open. For two centuries, almost everything that the family used or ate was produced at home under her direction. She spun and dyed the yarn that she wove into cloth and cut and hand-stitched into garments. She grew much of the food her family ate, and preserved enough to last the winter months. She made butter, cheese, bread, candles, and soap and knitted her family's stockings.[4]

In the <u>agrarian</u> economy of pre-industrial North America, a woman performing her household chores was thus a spinner, weaver and seamstress as well as a baker, butter-churner, candle-maker and soap-maker. And et cetera, et cetera, et cetera. As a matter of fact,

...the pressures of home production left very little time for the tasks that we would recognize today as housework. By all accounts, pre-industrial revolution women were sloppy housekeepers by today's standards. Instead of the daily cleaning or the weekly cleaning, there was the *spring* cleaning. Meals were simple and repetitive; clothes were changed infrequently; and the household wash was allowed to accumulate, and the washing done once a month, or in some households once in three months. And, of course, since each wash required the carting and heating of many buckets of water, higher standards of cleanliness were easily discouraged.[5]

10 Colonial women were not "house-cleaners" or "house-keepers" but rather full-fledged and accomplished workers within the home-based economy. Not only did they manufacture most of the products required by their families, they were also the guardians of their families' and their communities' health.

[1]Ann Oakley, *Woman's Work: The Housewife Past and Present* (New York: Vintage Books, 1976), p. 6.
[2]Barbara Ehrenreich and Deirdre English, "The Manufacture of Housework," in *Social Revolution*, no. 26, vol. 5, no. 5 (October–December 1975), p. 6.
[3]Frederick Engles, *Origin of the Family, Private Property and the State*, edited with an introduction by Eleanor Burke Leacock (New York: International Publishers, 1973). See Chapter 11. Leacock's introduction to this edition contains numerous enlightening observations on Engels' theory of the historical emergence of male supremacy.
[4]Barbara Wertheimer, *We Were There: The Story of Working Women in America* (New York: Pantheon Books, 1977), p. 12.
[5]Ehrenreich and English, *op cit.*, p. 10.

Starting Time	
Reading Time	
Finishing Time	
■ Reading Rate	

COMPREHENSION —

Read the following questions and statements. For each one, put an X in the box before the option that contains the most complete or accurate answer.

1. Frederick Engles argued that sexual inequality, as we know it today, did not exist before the dawn of
   □ a. women's liberation.
   □ b. private property.
   □ c. international travel.
   □ d. equal education.

2. We can generalize that the household duties that 20th-century women traditionally performed are looked upon by men as
   □ a. obtrusive.
   □ b. vital and extremely important.
   □ c. objectionable.
   □ d. minor and unimportant.

3. The first four paragraphs of this selection are organized to show
   □ a. a problem and a possible solution.
   □ b. spatial development.
   □ c. numerical facts.
   □ d. the steps in a process.

4. Choose the main idea of this passage.
   □ a. Working mothers find it increasingly difficult to manage both job and family.
   □ b. Housework has been looked at in many different ways by different groups of people at different times.
   □ c. Masai women are responsible for all aspects of domestic affairs.
   □ d. Modern conveniences have made housework less strenuous.

5. This article hints that the average housewife has generally been
   □ a. content and happy.
   □ b. mostly nonaggressive.
   □ c. totally unorganized.
   □ d. taken for granted.

6. Based on the selection, we can make the judgment that when it comes to housework, men have typically been
   - ☐ a. unhelpful.
   - ☐ b. realistic.
   - ☐ c. imaginative.
   - ☐ d. critical.

7. It would seem that the responsibilities within the Masai community
   - ☐ a. fall mainly upon the female population.
   - ☐ b. rest solely with the tribal males.
   - ☐ c. are equally shared among male and female.
   - ☐ d. are shared by both young and old.

8. The tone of this first paragraph can best be described as
   - ☐ a. being full of hope.
   - ☐ b. sentimental.
   - ☐ c. content.
   - ☐ d. expressing futility.

9. The writer reveals her attitudes through her
   - ☐ a. actions.
   - ☐ b. quotes.
   - ☐ c. comments.
   - ☐ d. appearance.

10. The writer uses the first paragraph to
   - ☐ a. define the nature of modern housework.
   - ☐ b. entertain the reader.
   - ☐ c. trace the history of housework.
   - ☐ d. present an unsolvable problem.

Comprehension Skills

1. recalling specific facts
2. retaining concepts
3. organizing facts
4. understanding the main idea
5. drawing a conclusion
6. making a judgment
7. making an inference
8. recognizing tone
9. understanding characters
10. appreciating literary forms

VOCABULARY, PART TWO —

Write the term that makes the most sense in each sentence.

unquantifiable   **arduously**
complementary   **hierarchical**
agrarian

1. The work of women has never been easy; they have always had to labor _____ at their tasks.

2. Most women cannot count the hours they put into housework, so it is _____ in terms of figuring out how much they could be paid for it.

3. Before most people lived in cities, when the country was more _____, there were few appliances to make housework easier.

4. But at that time the family seemed less _____; the husband was not automatically ranked over the wife.

5. Men and women each did their portion of the work, in a _____ manner.

enigmatically   **accessibility**
anathema   **obsolescence**
liquidate

6. When a new model of washer or dryer comes out, older models fall into _____.

7. Newer models have better control panels and other features that increase their _____.

8. Stores carrying only the older models often cannot sell them and so have to _____ their stock.

9. Most women cannot figure out where their time goes when they are working; it seems to disappear

_____ .

10. For many women housework is

_____ ; they hate it more than anything.

Comprehension Score   [_____]

Vocabulary Score   [_____]

WRITING —

Davis wrote this selection on housework over 15 years ago. To what extent do you think housework is still mainly a woman's job? Have men become more involved? Write a few paragraphs expressing your opinion. Use specific examples from your own experience to support what you say.

STUDY SKILLS —

Read the following passage and answer the questions that follow it.

Contextual Aids, III

6. Synonyms. Many times, unfamiliar words can be understood by noticing synonyms provided in the context. A synonym, as you recall, is a word with the same or nearly the same meaning as another word. Readers have the task of recognizing that a synonym is being given. With this knowledge, they can properly use the contextual aid. For example, a student reading the sentence *It was his custom never to be on time: he made a _____ of tardiness* must recognize that the missing word is a synonym for *custom*. The word *habit* instantly comes to mind, completing the sentence perfectly. This contextual aid is often found in textbook writing.

7. Setting the Mood. The setting or mood created by the context can suggest to the reader the meaning of an unfamiliar word. In the sentence *It was a lovely _____ scene, with snow blanketing the fields and trees,* the set-

ting is obviously *winter*. This would appear to be the word indicated by the context. Using setting and mood effectively requires imagery comprehension; the reader must get the feeling or tone. Highly descriptive writing and poetry are filled with this type of contextual aid.

8. Association. Certain words can arouse associations in the mind of the reader. These, in turn, serve as aids in order to recognize an unfamiliar word. The student reading the sentence *Tuning their instruments, the _____ awaited the appearance of the conductor* can see that the missing word is probably *musicians, band,* or *orchestra.* The words *tuning, instruments,* and *conductor* trigger the correct associations. The context of much of what we read provides opportunities for making associations like these.

1. A synonym is a word with the

_____ meaning as another

word.

2. Context sometimes creates a

_____ or mood that can be

used as a contextual aid.

3. For example, after criticizing capitalist society in paragraph 4, you would expect Davis's next statement, that "industrialized housework—like all unprofitable enterprises, is *anathema*" to that economy, would continue in that critical

_____ .

4. Certain words trigger _____ in the mind of the reader that serve as aids in recognizing unknown words.

5. For instance, if you did not know the word *accumulate* in Davis's statement "the household wash was allowed to accumulate, and the washing done once a month" the phrase _____ would help you understand its meaning.

12

A Touch of Innocence

Katherine Dunham

AUTHOR NOTES—
Katherine Dunham, born in 1910, achieved fame for her contributions to the world of dance; she was among the first to recognize black dance as art. Educated as an anthropologist at The University of Chicago and Northwestern University, Dunham went on to direct and teach her own schools of dance, theater, and cultural arts worldwide. One of her favorite projects has been working with the Performing Arts Training Center in the predominantly black city of East St. Louis, Illinois. Dunham has also been an artist-in-residence at the University of Illinois.

Dunham has published books with subject matter ranging from fantasy to autobiography to nonfiction. She has also been involved in many aspects of the film and television business, including television scriptwriting.

VOCABULARY, PART ONE—
All of these terms are in the story you are about to read. Study each term and its meaning. Then answer the questions below.

As you read the story, notice how each vocabulary term is used. You will have more questions about the terms later.

echelon, level of authority or rank

wield, exert with authority; control

elation, great joy or pride

auspicious, promising success; favorable

confounding, confusing

tyranny, cruel use of power

morbid, not normal or healthy

nocturnal, occurring at night

sacrosanct, sacred; holy

aplomb, self-assurance

1. Which word might name a child's feelings on the last day of school?

   _____

2. Which word describes what three good job recommendations could be regarded as?

   _____

3. Which word describes the kind of activities that animals who sleep during the day

   usually engage in? _____

4. Which word could describe a person's curiosity about a place where a brutal murder

   has been committed? _____

5. Which word could identify the quality of a person who has a strong belief that she

   will do well on a job? _____

A READING PURPOSE—

In this selection Katherine Dunham begins a job and seems not to understand the reactions of the people around her. Read to see what you can make of their reactions.

---

1 Hamilton Park Branch Library was located in an upper middle-class suburban district of the City where Jews were unwelcome, foreigners of less than two-generation citizenship scarce, and Negroes unknown except as part-time hired help. As for the McLaughlin sisters, they were in the highest eche-lon of the City's librarians. They were small, neatly formed, soft-spoken Irish spinsters, separated in age by seven or eight years, but so much alike in looks, dress, and manner that patrons of the branch where Bernardine might be stationed would at some other branch immediately recognize Blanche as her kin. Bernardine, the elder of the two, governed not only the tastes and behavior of her sister, but was believed by most of the librarians junior to her to wield an influence over the political structure of the library system comparable to that wielded by her countrymen in the City's politics in general.

2 When Katherine Dunham descended from the street-car that had taken her, after a series of transfers, from the apartment her brother had found for her to the quiet, tree-shaded avenue ending at Hamilton Park, her heart was in her mouth and her knees were weak; but she felt a great sense of elation, convinced that the most difficult hurdles of her life lay behind her. The past having been accomplished, the future could hold no terrors. She had been granted permission by the college to matriculate in

■ *absentia,* and she had passed the Civil Service examination with a high enough rating to win a place in what was considered one of the best-run and most desirable branch libraries of the City. She was innocent about what this might mean, but her niece, who had failed to pass the same examination, assured her that she had been very fortunate indeed.

3 If she noticed that Bernardine McLaughlin's smile was a little frozen, she must have thought this proper in one occupying the post of head librarian in an important branch. If the other young women, junior and senior assistants, regarded her with open curiosity but acknowledged her name with only a slight nod, then this must be customary on such auspicious occasions. She, Katherine Dunham, by some miracle still confounding her, had in one grand movement left behind the Town, the West Side Cleaners and Dyers, the flat on Bluff Street, the cottage on Elmwood Avenue, the unawareness of her mother, the tyranny of her father, corporal punishment, financial insecurity, the disintegration of the dust wheel, the morbid attraction of the quarry, the loneliness of the room with the single star piercing its window, the uncertainties of her questing childhood and defeated adolescence.

4 If her new colleagues—of Irish and Scotch and Italian and Polish and just plain American heritage—

did not at first recognize her as one of them, that would come later. They were looking at her so strangely because she had come from somewhere else, and it would take time to know one another, as it had in grade school and high school and junior college. If the patrons regarded her strangely, it was because they must sense her amazement at what had happened to her, must even be wishing that they, too, could enter into this magical state of frightened exaltation. As she turned from her locker to her first duty, she felt suddenly alone, but she quickly recovered, reasoning that it was no more than just that her guiding spirit be given a respite. The rows of books were familiar and comforting, and by noon of the first day she had mastered the simple routine of entering and discharging books, even of selecting them by catalogue number.

5 It did not seem at all strange that the head librarian held a meeting around the polished round oak table in the inner reading room, barring all patrons for the time and excluding her alone of the staff. She sat on a high stool at the front desk with ink pads, date stamps, filing cards, and returned books neatly arranged before her. Her innocence went so far as to leave her all unsuspecting when, immediately after the meeting, a new schedule of lunch hours was posted and a third period was instituted for her name, which had earlier been grouped with several others. Because she knew no one, this meant little to her.

6 When the time came for her special lunch hour, she relinquished her position at the front desk to a dark-haired, sparkling-eyed girl named Florence Hazzard and received in return a warm smile, her first of the day. The smile was a little pitying, too, but she didn't know that.

7 The late spring air was warm, and she walked out of the park into shaded avenues that reminded her of Delavan and her morning walks with her Uncle Ed as she had first known him. She wandered along

> For Katherine, a new job and a new life were ahead, trouble was behind...or so she thought.

several thoroughfares lined with budding shrubbery, but with no sign of a restaurant or lunch room. She wondered vaguely where the other girls had eaten lunch, whether they all lived in the neighborhood. Before her hour was over, she returned to the park and sat on a stone bench not far from the low building housing the library. She could see Bernardine McLaughlin bent over the typewriter on the desk of her private office, and watched her for some time, wondering what document so absorbed the attention of the head librarian and if she always bit her under lip when she typed.

8 Suddenly she remembered that she was hungry and resolved to bring her lunch the following day, wondering if it would be the right thing to do and if any of the other girls brought lunches. She wondered, too, what would happen in wintertime, whether then she would sit like this in the park by herself. The invisible figure of her <u>nocturnal</u> excursions drew closer, protecting her from learning too soon about the conspiracies at that moment under way. But even if she had known the startling effect of her innocent descent upon the heretofore <u>sacrosanct</u> confines, she might have accepted it with complete <u>aplomb</u>.

9 The great wide world opened before her. Her lunch hour was over, and she went inside.

Starting Time [ ]

Reading Time [ ]

Finishing Time [ ]

■ Reading Rate [ ]

COMPREHENSION —
Read the following questions and statements. For each one, put an X in the box before the option that contains the most complete or accurate answer.

1. The author of the selection used to take morning walks with her
   - ☐ a. father.
   - ☐ b. brother.
   - ☐ c. uncle.
   - ☐ d. nephew.

2. The third paragraph suggests that Katherine Dunham
   - ☐ a. has suffered many hardships.
   - ☐ b. can no longer deal with reality.
   - ☐ c. will soon be fired from her job.
   - ☐ d. cannot endure emotional pressure.

3. In this selection, the writer uses
   - ☐ a. simple listings.
   - ☐ b. time order.
   - ☐ c. cause and effect.
   - ☐ d. comparison and contrast.

4. Which of the following old sayings best states the main thought of this passage?
   - ☐ a. Gone but not forgotten
   - ☐ b. Here today, gone tomorrow
   - ☐ c. Ignorance is bliss
   - ☐ d. Out of sight, out of mind

5. This selection hints that Bernardine
   - ☐ a. hated her younger sister.
   - ☐ b. protected her younger sister.
   - ☐ c. ignored her younger sister.
   - ☐ d. dominated her younger sister.

6. The fact that the McLaughlin sisters were librarians indicates that
   - ☐ a. they were college graduates.
   - ☐ b. many people trusted them.
   - ☐ c. politicians welcomed their support.
   - ☐ d. minorities respected their position.

7. We can make the judgment that Bernardine
   - ☐ a. really liked Katherine.
   - ☐ b. intended to make things difficult for Katherine.
   - ☐ c. had been instrumental in bringing Katherine to the library.
   - ☐ d. disliked all the library workers.

8. The tone of this selection is built around the
   - ☐ a. actions of the librarians.
   - ☐ b. opinions of the writer.
   - ☐ c. description of the library.
   - ☐ d. excitement of the reader.

9. From this article, one would guess that Bernardine is
   - ☐ a. modest.
   - ☐ b. sympathetic.
   - ☐ c. generous.
   - ☐ d. unfriendly.

10. Paragraph 7 appeals to the reader's sense of
    - ☐ a. sound.
    - ☐ b. sight.
    - ☐ c. touch.
    - ☐ d. taste.

Comprehension Skills
1. recalling specific facts
2. retaining concepts
3. organizing facts
4. understanding the main idea
5. drawing a conclusion
6. making a judgment
7. making an inference
8. recognizing tone
9. understanding characters
10. appreciating literary forms

VOCABULARY, PART TWO —
Write the term that makes the most sense in each sentence.

echelon   elation
auspicious   tyranny
aplomb

1. Katherine felt a great sense of

   _____ about beginning her

   new job; she was so excited she could hardly wait

   to start.

2. Though she did not have a great deal of self-confi-

   dence, she tried to approach her tasks with as much

   _____ as she could.

3. The woman she was to work for was, naturally, of a

   higher _____ than Katherine.

4. Katherine would find out later that this woman used _____ rather than kindness in dealing with her employees.

5. Nevertheless, a bright, sunny day and not having to wait at all for a bus seemed to be _____ signs of good things to come.

morbid   nocturnal
sacrosanct   confounding
wield

6. Katherine's employer was known to _____ an influence over the political structure of the library.

7. Her office was considered _____; no one could enter without a special invitation,

8. Some thought that this woman's _____ activities, done after daylight was gone, were a little strange.

9. Her extremely close relationship with her sister was also thought to be a bit _____.

10. Katherine found the stories about the woman to be _____ and did not know what to make of them.

Comprehension Score   [   ]

Vocabulary Score   [   ]

W R I T I N G —

What do you think will happen to Katherine on this job? Write a few paragraphs that explain the way you think the other workers will treat her, based on what you inferred from the story. If you want, you can include an incident that might have happened between Katherine and one or more of the others.

S T U D Y   S K I L L S —
Read the following passage and answer the questions that follow it.

Contextual Aids, IV
9. Adjective Clauses. New words can be understood when accompanied by adjective clauses. Frequently an unknown word modified by an adjective clause can be understood by the information contained in the clause. In the sentence *The _____ which shine in the sky at the night have always fascinated people,* the missing word is modified by an adjective clause. The same clause acts as a contextual aid, telling the reader that the missing word is *stars.*

10. Appositives. A word can be recognized and understood through another word used in apposition to it. A word in apposition is placed beside a word, further explaining it. Appositives give the reader a clue to the meaning of the unknown word. In the sentence _____ , *policemen in plain clothes, joined the investigation,* the reader is informed by the appositive *policemen in plain clothes* that the missing word is probably *detectives.* Appositives are always placed just before or after the word they explain. For this reason they are relatively easy to recognize and exploit as contextual aids.

11. Cause and Effect. Words can be understood through a cause-and-effect relationship between the unknown word and other words in the sentence. The reader's understanding of the cause-and-effect pattern offers a clue to the meaning of the unknown word. In the sentence *Because they ate a hearty lunch just before swimming, many of the bathers suffered _____ , anyone who understands the effect of eating just before swimming knows that the missing word is *cramps.*

Discovering word meaning through context clues is not new to you; you have been using context intuitively all your life. However, as you encounter more and more difficult words with subtle or complex meanings, you will come to realize that the use of context clues is one of your most powerful learning tools.

1. New words can sometimes be understood from information contained in _____ clauses.

2. Another contextual aid is a word in _____ placed next to the unknown word.

3. Appositives _____ explain the words placed next to them.

4. Sometimes a reader's understanding of a _____ -effect pattern can help to clarify the meaning of an unknown word.

5. For example, in the statement "she felt a great sense of *elation,* convinced that the most difficult hurdles of her life lay behind her," the _____ of overcoming difficulties would clearly be happiness, or elation.

13 | Fatheralong

John Edgar Wideman

AUTHOR NOTES—

John Edgar Wideman spent his first ten years in the rough Homewood area of Pittsburgh, Pennsylvania, and began writing as a student at the University of Pennsylvania. In 1963, Wideman became the second African American to win a Rhodes Scholarship to Oxford University, taking a degree in philosophy. He has taught African American studies at the University of Pennsylvania and University of Wyoming in Laramie and currently teaches in the English department of the University of Massachusetts in Amherst.

Wideman's books include the nonfiction *Brothers and Keepers* and *Fatheralong;* several novels, including *Sent for You Yesterday*, a PEN/Faulkner Award winner and the third in his highly regarded Homewood Trilogy; and short story collections. He also contributes articles, stories, book reviews, and poetry to various periodicals.

VOCABULARY, PART ONE—

All of these terms are in the story you are about to read. Study each term and its meaning. Then answer the questions below.

As you read the story, notice how each vocabulary term is used. You will have more questions about the terms later.

animated, brought to life

compressed, squeezed tightly together

prerogatives, rights; privileges

disinterring, digging up something that is buried

vestige, trace

imponderable, unable to be precisely measured or evaluated

severed, cut off

unprecedented, never done or known before

meticulously, carefully; exactly

presumption, cause or reason for believing something

1. Which word describes what robbers might be doing digging in a cemetery at night?

   _____

2. Which word tells what happened to a huge branch that was removed from a tree?

   _____

3. Which word tells what a cartoonist did with the characters she drew?

   _____

4. Which word could describe how a person works who pays very precise attention to

   details? _____

5. Which word might a person use in describing the first time a three-way tie in an

   election ever happened in his organization? _____

A READING PURPOSE—

In this selection Wideman, who has gone back to the South with his father searching for information about their ancestors, visits the town where the local historical archives are kept. As you read, put yourself in Wideman's place and try to understand his feelings.

_____

1   In the bookshop off the town square of Abbeville I had found none of my books. I might have attributed this shutout to the shadow of the Confederate monument in the plaza at the square's center, except more often than not, Yankee or Confederate, east or west, most bookshops didn't stock my stuff. What was unusual was the owner's regret after I identified myself as a writer with roots in the region, her admission that she wasn't familiar with my work, her assurance she'd remedy what she declared to be an unfortunate, even embarrassing oversight. She also offered to call her friend, a former professor of history at a local college who happened to be the author of a book about Abbeville, and enlist his assistance in the project that had brought my father and myself to town. Her kindness and generosity in introducing the man, his book, sharing her extensive library of local lore—books, maps, pamphlets, reprints, catalogues—were matched by the retired professor's enthusiastic response to her suggestion. Over the course of a few days he taught me in hours what might have taken me weeks to sort out on my own. I learned where and how to use some of the research materials he'd spent a good part of his life poring over. Bowie Lomax epitomized, without being stuffy, condescending, or boring, the English ideal of country gentleman and scholar. Retaining in his manner a bit of the inspired amateur, leavened with an academic's discipline and fussiness, he animated Abbeville with stories and facts. As I strolled around the square with him, literally, or in the tales he narrated while we shared a meal, every building, tree, crossroads, possessed a soul, a life history to be gleaned if you acquainted yourself with its special language. The imagination of Bowie Lomax moved in Great Time, past, present, and future simultaneously.

2   I'd enjoyed his company, benefitted incalculably from his patient tutelage, his stores of information as he conveyed to me the mysteries and mechanics of using Platt books, indexes, cartridge-case-like boxes of wills that had recorded property transactions in the county since before the Revolutionary War. I was grateful, even fond of this elderly man who shared himself, his insights and craft, so unreservedly with a stranger, and that's why I was surprised, shocked even, by the ice-cold wave of anger, the fury compressed into one of those if-looks-could-kill looks I found myself flashing down at the back of his thin, freckled bald skull.

3   From my perch on a ladder as Bowie Lomax read their serial numbers from a king-sized ledger, I was passing down metal boxes stuffed with ancient wills, letters, bills of sale, itemized appraisals of real estate and personal property that were required to

legally convey wealth from the dead hand to the living. While the professor led me through the process of unearthing our shared past, my father sat outside the courthouse, basking in the sun on a

> Slavery had been outlawed over 140 years ago. But it seemed to John Edgar Wideman that some of its effects would never go away.

bench in the restored square of Abbeville. The unanticipated glare of pure animosity had a lot to do with my father, I'm sure. He was about the same age as Bowie Lomax, as smart, as curious and engaging. Yet, because of his color, my father had been denied the prospects, the possibilities that had enriched the career and life of the white man below me.

4 Quickly, I realized I felt no desire to actually harm Bowie Lomax, but damage had been done. A silent apology issued from me almost simultaneous with the explosion of hostility. Nothing personal. Nothing about you, my new friend.

5 However, the urge to strike, to destroy, wasn't totally abstract, either. It was Professor Lomax's skull I had envisioned shattering, spilling all its learning, its intimate knowledge of these deeds that transferred in the same "livestock" column as cows, horses, and mules, the bodies of my ancestors from one white owner to another. Hadn't the historian's career been one more mode of appropriation and exploitation of my father's bones, the pearls that were his eyes. Didn't mastery of Abbeville's history, the power and privilege to tell my father's story, follow from the original sin of slavery that stole, then silenced, my father's voice. The professor was a bona fide expert. He'd earned a living studying, passing on, institutionalizing what he knew about us, including how we were bought and sold, how a region flourished based upon trafficking in human souls. Not only flourished, but attempted to legitimize and preserve its prerogatives for all the world to see

with these crumbling pieces of paper we were disinterring.

6 I wanted the room to disappear, the hardy, vital old man to disappear, every vestige of the complacent, unrepentant reality of slavery to be scoured from the earth. My rage was not meant for my companion in that musty room crammed wall to wall, floor to ceiling, with decaying documents. What I wanted was another chance for my father. I wanted this air cleared for a different world, not so my father would be Bowie Lomax, not so Bowie Lomax would be struck down and made to suffer for the crimes of his fathers. I didn't know what kind of world, what kind of life I wished for my father or the professor or what they might wish for themselves. What should come next is always imponderable, always problematic, but I knew in that moment my anger flashed we had not severed ourselves from a version of history that had made the lives of my black father and this white man so separate, so distant, yet so intimately intertwined.

7 Upon a stepladder in the probate-office storage vault in Abbeville, South Carolina, I had experienced with unprecedented immediacy the fact of slavery. A grave full of chained skeletons wouldn't have been more convincing. In this room there was no denying the solid, banal, everyday business-as-usual role slavery played in America's past. Meticulously, unashamedly, the perpetrators had preserved evidence of their crimes. Given their practice the official stamp of approval. Not only did a world that once had been, shove its reality into my face, these documents also confirmed how much the present, my father's life, mine, yours, are still being determined by the presumption of white over black inscribed in them.

Starting Time

Reading Time

Finishing Time

■ Reading Rate

COMPREHENSION —

Read the following questions and statements. For each one, put an X in the box before the option that contains the most complete or accurate answer.

1. The town that Wideman is visiting is named
   - ☐ a. Greenwood.
   - ☐ b. Abbeville.
   - ☐ c. Bowie.
   - ☐ d. Charlotte.

2. Wideman's father didn't have the same opportunities as Professor Lomax because
   - ☐ a. he wasn't smart enough to go to college.
   - ☐ b. he became a father at an early age.
   - ☐ c. he had only wanted outdoor jobs.
   - ☐ d. he was black.

3. This entire selection is built around
   - ☐ a. a file.
   - ☐ b. a book of photographs.
   - ☐ c. an "if-looks-could-kill" look.
   - ☐ d. the Confederate monument in the town square.

4. One of this main points that Wideman makes in this selection is
   - ☐ a. whites can be outwardly nice to blacks but still hate them underneath.
   - ☐ b. the remnants of slavery are still there to hold blacks back.
   - ☐ c. the South is the only place in America where you can find records like those he examined.
   - ☐ d. it is foolish to get angry when you can't change a situation.

5. Lomax had benefited from slavery because he
   - ☐ a. had learned to give better treatment to the blacks he knew.
   - ☐ b. helped the town set up tours of old plantations.
   - ☐ c. had gotten a job Wideman's father should have gotten.
   - ☐ d. made his living doing historical interpretation of old slave records.

6. The first paragraph of this selection leads you to believe that Wideman
   - ☐ a. feels a lot of anger toward the people he meets.
   - ☐ b. will not be staying in the town very long.
   - ☐ c. will be telling about a pleasant event.
   - ☐ d. has forced his father to make the trip with him.

7. Lomax's reaction to Wideman's anger
   - ☐ a. is to respond in his usual gracious way.
   - ☐ b. is to be sad that Wideman doesn't appreciate his efforts.
   - ☐ c. never comes: he doesn't even know Wideman is angry.
   - ☐ d. is to get angry himself.

8. The tone of the selection
   - ☐ a. begins to change in the second paragraph.
   - ☐ b. remains the same throughout.
   - ☐ c. begins to change in the last paragraph.
   - ☐ d. alternates between contentment and rage in each paragraph.

9. Lomax was a man who
   - ☐ a. liked to pretend that slavery had had no effect on blacks.
   - ☐ b. tried to be helpful rather than offensive.
   - ☐ c. had grown up in the North but later moved to the South.
   - ☐ d. demonstrated strong feelings of bigotry.

10. This selection is taken from a
    - ☐ a. novel set in the present.
    - ☐ b. novel set in historical times.
    - ☐ c. book of nonfiction.
    - ☐ d. short story.

Comprehension Skills
1. recalling specific facts
2. retaining concepts
3. organizing facts
4. understanding the main idea
5. drawing a conclusion
6. making a judgment
7. making an inference
8. recognizing tone
9. understanding characters
10. appreciating literary forms

VOCABULARY, PART TWO —
Write the term that makes the most sense in each sentence.

meticulously **compressed**
disinterring **vestige**
unprecedented

1. By _____ old county records, Wideman hoped to find information that was buried in them.

2. He was looking for some _____ of his family's history, some thread of information to help him understand the past.

3. His search was _____ in that county; no blacks had tried to check their history in that way before.

4. He found years and years of records _____ tightly into small files.

5. By taking his time and searching _____, he could find just what he wanted.

presumption **imponderable**
severed **prerogatives**
animated

6. Dry, dead history was _____ by the records Wideman found; people and events seemed to jump to life off the pages.

7. It was clear that blacks had been _____ from white society and not allowed to participate in it.

8. Though he could not exactly define all the effects of slavery, he knew they were doing _____ harm to many present-day blacks.

9. Whites' _____ that they were superior to blacks was one result of slavery.

10. Their expectation of getting good jobs and housing and other similar _____ was another result.

Comprehension Score [ ]

Vocabulary Score [ ]

WRITING —
What do you think Professor Lomax would say to Wideman if Wideman explained why he was angry? Writing as Lomax, compose a few paragraphs of response to Wideman. Make your response fit in with Lomax's character as it is presented in the selection.

STUDY SKILLS —
Read the following passage and answer the questions that follow it.

Reviewing for Examinations, I
For many students, the expression "into every life a little rain must fall" pertains to taking final examinations. Although many schools are revising the portion of final grades based on examinations, most students will still be taking exams for most courses. They are a fact of academic life.

Unfortunately (and unnecessarily), many students panic at examination time. They worry so much that they cannot study and review effectively. This results in poor performance on the test and then even more apprehension on future tests. If you are one of these people, you must break the cycle. Success on your next set of finals can reverse the process.

The main reason students panic is lack of adequate preparation. To most students, final review means cramming—a do or die, headlong plunge into the unfamiliar waters of the subject matter. Cramming can be beneficial; any brief, intensive review is sure to do more good than harm. As your only method of exam preparation, however, cramming lets you down. There's just too much to be covered.

Successful preparation has two prerequisites: suitable notes and continuous review. You cannot begin to study well with unsatisfactory notes. In addition to knowing what is in the text, you must be able to recall and review what was emphasized in class. You need a good set of notes to do this.

You must review regularly and faithfully all through the term, not just before exams. This approach will not only ease the load at exam time, but will also lead to a better understanding of the subject matter with each review.

1. Successful examination preparation includes good

    _____ and continuous review.

2. Too much worry can result in poor

    _____ results.

3. Cramming should not be your only

    _____ of test preparation.

4. In addition to material from the text, you must review important notes from _____.

5. Better understanding of the subject matter is accomplished with each _____.

The Glory Trumpeter

14

Derek Walcott

AUTHOR NOTES—
Derek Walcott was born in 1930 on the island of St. Lucia in the West Indies. He has written plays and poems that deal with life and culture in the Caribbean Islands. Walcott has been a teacher as well as a student of drama and now lives in both Trinidad and New York. In 1992 he received the Nobel Prize for literature.

Walcott's first book of poetry, *Twenty-Five Poems,* was published when he was only 18. Another early work, *In A Green Night: Poems 1948-1960,* is concerned mostly with the natural beauty of his homeland. Some of his later collections, such as *The Fortunate Traveller* and *Midsummer,* deal with moving away from the Caribbean and learning to live in other places. One of Walcott's most famous poems is the 1990 "Omeros," a book-length work that puts the stories of the Greek poet Homer into a Caribbean setting.

VOCABULARY, PART ONE—
All of these terms are in the story you are about to read. Study each term and its meaning. Then answer the questions below.

As you read the story, notice how each vocabulary term is used. You will have more questions about the terms later.

derisive, ridiculing; mocking

avuncular, like an uncle

fixed, stared at

sallow, sickly or yellowish color

lean, thin

compliant, agreeable; willing to go along with things

funereal, gloomy; melancholy

homburgs, man's soft felt hats with rolled brims

fêting, celebrating

meted, portioned out; distributed

1. Which word could describe a person so scrawny-looking that all his clothes seem to fall off him? _____

2. Which word could describe the atmosphere at a gathering where everyone seems sad and depressed? _____

3. Which word might describe someone who is always willing to adjust her plans so they will fit in better with yours? _____

4. Which word might tell what you are doing if you are enjoying yourself at a friend's birthday party? _____

5. Which word might describe the skin of someone who is ill?

_____

A READING PURPOSE —

This selection deals with a Caribbean musician who has returned to his homeland from the United States. As you read, try to decide what his feelings are.

_____

■

    Old Eddie's face, wrinkled with river lights,
    Looked like a Mississippi man's. The eyes,
    <u>Derisive</u> and <u>avuncular</u> at once,
    Swivelling, <u>fixed</u> me. They'd seen
5   Too many wakes, too many cathouse nights.
    The bony, idle fingers on the valves
    Of his knee-cradled horn could tear
    Through "Georgia on My Mind" or "Jesus Saves"
    With the same fury of indifference
10 If what propelled such frenzy was despair.

    Now, as the eyes sealed in the ashen flesh,
    And Eddie, like a deacon at his prayer,
    Rose, tilting the bright horn, I saw a flash
    Of gulls and pigeons from the dunes of coal
15 Near my grandmother's barracks on the wharves,
    I saw the <u>sallow</u> faces of those men
    Who sighed as if they spoke into their graves
    About the Negro in America. That was when
    The Sunday comics, sprawled out on her floor,
20 Sent from the States, had a particular odour;
    Dry smell of money mingled with man's sweat.

And yet, if Eddie's features held our fate,
Secure in childhood I did not know then
A jesus-ragtime or gut-bucket blues
25 To the bowed heads of <u>lean</u>, <u>compliant</u> men
Back from the States in their <u>funereal</u> serge,
Black, rusty <u>homburgs</u> and limp waiters' ties,
Slow, honey accents and lard-coloured eyes,
Was Joshua's ram's horn wailing for the Jews
30 Of patient bitterness or bitter siege.

Now it was that, as Eddie turned his back
On our young crowd out <u>fêting</u>, swilling liquor,
And blew, eyes closed, one foot up, out to sea,
His horn aimed at those cities of the Gulf,
35 Mobile and Galveston, and sweetly <u>meted</u>
Their horn of plenty through his bitter cup,
In lonely exaltation blaming me
For all whom race and exile have defeated,
For my own uncle in America,
40 That living there I never could look up.

Starting Time	
Reading Time	
Finishing Time	
Reading Rate	

■

C O M P R E H E N S I O N —

Read the following questions and statements. For each one, put an X in the box before the option that contains the most complete or accurate answer.

1. The instrument that Eddie played was a
   □ a. piano.
   □ b. fiddle.
   □ c. saxophone.
   □ d. trumpet.

2. The narrator of the poem is
   □ a. a member of Eddie's band.
   □ b. a young man listening to Eddie's music.
   □ c. Eddie's grandmother.
   □ d. a group of tourists from Galveston.

3. The events in the second stanza, from line 13 on,
   □ a. are the narrator's memories and childhood recollections.
   □ b. tell how Eddie felt as a child.
   □ c. are things happening while Eddie is playing.
   □ d. show how fond the grandmother was of the musicians.

4. Which of these lines refers to the attitudes of many musicians who returned from America?
   □ a. "Slow, honey accents and lard-coloured eyes"
   □ b. "The Sunday comics, sprawled out on her floor"
   □ c. "The bony, idle fingers on the valves"
   □ d. "...all whom race and exile have defeated"

5. Eddie's reaction to the choice of different songs he plays is
   ☐ a. enthusiasm.
   ☐ b. indifference.
   ☐ c. amusement.
   ☐ d. anger.

6. In the Bible, Joshua's horn blew and knocked down the walls of cities the Jews were conquering. In the poem, the musicians wanted to conquer
   ☐ a. cities in Biblical lands.
   ☐ b. cities in their native islands.
   ☐ c. cities along the Gulf of Mexico.
   ☐ d. cities in Canada.

7. A main conflict for musicians like Eddie is
   ☐ a. wanting to be better players but not having the talent.
   ☐ b. hating the other musicians they play with.
   ☐ c. feeling that audiences don't appreciate them.
   ☐ d. resenting the United States yet longing to be there.

8. The music played by Eddie creates a feeling of
   ☐ a. happiness and good humor.
   ☐ b. sadness and desire.
   ☐ c. anger and rage.
   ☐ d. success and glory.

9. The musicians the poem describes
   ☐ a. have always known success.
   ☐ b. are young enough to make important changes in their lives.
   ☐ c. frequently feel sorry for themselves.
   ☐ d. are more or less accepting of their fate.

10. Describing Eddie playing as "like a deacon at his prayer" is an example of
    ☐ a. literal comparison.
    ☐ b. simile.
    ☐ c. metaphor.
    ☐ d. personification.

Comprehension Skills

1. recalling specific facts
2. retaining concepts
3. organizing facts
4. understanding the main idea
5. drawing a conclusion
6. making a judgment
7. making an inference
8. recognizing tone
9. understanding characters
10. appreciating literary forms

VOCABULARY, PART TWO —

Write the term that makes the most sense in each sentence.

derisive	sallow
lean	compliant
homburgs	

1. The men in the band were

   _____; they would play any

   song the audience asked for.

2. A few of the players were overweight, but most of

   them were _____.

3. They wore cheap suits on their backs and

   _____ on their heads.

4. Most of the players had very dark skin, but Eddie's

   was rather _____.

5. His _____ smile could make

   you believe he was making fun of you.

avuncular	funereal
fêting	meted
fixed	

6. If you were out _____, this

   band could keep you in a good mood.

7. They _____ out their sweet

   songs fairly—one for you, one for someone else in

   the audience.

8. If you were feeling sad, they could complement

   your mood with a _____ song.

9. The _____ smile of the oldest

   band member could make you feel he was one of

   your family.

10. If he _____ his gaze on you,

    his steady look was always accompanied by a grin.

Comprehension Score [   ]

Vocabulary Score [   ]

WRITING —

What are some of the songs you think Eddie might be playing? Write down the titles of these songs. For each song, write a sentence or two that explains why he might have played them. Base your ideas on what you know about Eddie's attitudes from the poem.

STUDY SKILLS —

Read the following passage and answer the questions that follow it.

Reviewing for Examinations, II

Reviewing sounds like a lot of extra work, but it actually makes your life much easier. By keeping up with your work, you are more relaxed and more confident. You will actually save time in the long run.

If you have not been reviewing during the term, start now. It will probably be necessary for you to outline the course to date; this is the best way to be sure you have covered everything. Schedule a week for the task and review and outline a segment each night. Anticipate as much reviewing as possible now.

With these two conditions in order, you are ready to get down to the business of studying for final exams.

STUDYING FOR FINALS

1. Establishing a Review Schedule. As you have learned from working with your regular study schedule, you must be organized to study successfully. Set up a new schedule a week or two before final exams, spreading the material to be reviewed and studied over the allotted time. Save the final day or evening (the one before the actual test) for cramming; you will learn later how to cram intelli-gently. Divide the course work among the other days so that every aspect of the subject can be covered.

Assign a reasonable length of time to your daily study period. If a subject is one of your "good" ones, an hour a day of concentrated study might be sufficient. If, on the other hand, a subject has been giving you trouble, you will need to devote more time to it. Schedule accordingly.

Draw up your review schedule on paper, showing the time allotment each day for the subject. Obviously, for the system to work, you must spend the full time in actual study.

1. The best way to be sure you cover everything in a review is to _____ the course to date.

2. When you set up your study schedule, _____ the material to be reviewed over the allotted time.

3. If a subject has been giving you trouble, you will need to devote more _____ to it.

4. For instance, if you find reading _____ like those of Derek Walcott more difficult than reading prose, you should adjust your schedule accordingly.

5. The full time planned for review each day must be spent in actual _____.

15

Showing My Color

Clarence Page

AUTHOR NOTES—
Clarence Page is a Pulitzer Prize-winning journalist and television commentator who deals with African American issues as well as many other topics. His regular column, which is syndicated by the *Chicago Tribune*, appears in over one hundred American newspapers; he has also written for the *New Republic* and *The Wall Street Journal*. Page frequently offers insightful commentary on such programs as National Public Radio's *Sunday Morning Edition* and PBS's *The MacLaughlin Group*. He presently lives in Maryland.

VOCABULARY, PART ONE—
All of these terms are in the story you are about to read. Study each term and its meaning. Then answer the questions below.

As you read the story, notice how each vocabulary term is used. You will have more questions about the terms later.

susceptible, likely to be affected by

chaotic, disordered; out of control

paradox, statement that is true but seems to say impossible things

zealot, strong believer; fanatic

heretic, person who no longer believes all the doctrines of a religion or cause

stridency, shrill, irritating speech or behavior

gravitate, move or be pulled toward

pragmatic, practical; down to earth

regress, move in a backward direction

transcends, goes beyond; surpasses

1. Which word tells what children do when they forget over the summer much of what they learned in the past school year? _____

2. Which word describes a decision based not on theory but on everyday experience?

   _____

3. Which word describes the condition of a classroom where all the children are running around wildly? _____

4. Which word could name a person who stands on street corners preaching that people should repent because the end of the world is coming?

   _____

5. Which word might identify a statement like "The blind man sees more clearly than anyone else here"? _____

A READING PURPOSE —

In this selection Clarence Page gives his views on the various ways blacks relate to their racial identity and the world around them. As you read, decide whether or not you think his ideas are accurate.

1   "There is an oversimplification of the Negro," Zora Neale Hurston said in a 1944 interview with the New York *Amsterdam News*. "He is either pictured by conservatives as happy, picking his banjo, or by the so-called liberals as low, miserable and crying. The Negro's life is neither of these. Rather, it is in-between and above and below these pictures."

2   The world has changed much since then, but the oversimplification of the African American persists. We are either victims, as Jesse Jackson portrays us, or just "vulnerable," as Shelby Steel describes us, with not much in between. We hate ourselves, as a consequence of having been indoctrinated and convinced by white racist standards of beauty and intelligence, or we love ourselves too much, a consequence of overcompensation for our "wound-edness."

3   Our reality is far more complicated, more complicated than even most black people realize. Too many of us speak and behave, for example, as if there is only one way to be "black." In fact, there are many ways. It is only our sense of insecurity that attempts to suppress the individuality of those who would wander off the plantation.

4   Black people, like other people, come in all varieties, and we go through changes. There are, for example, the racial innocents, who have little or no sense of racial identity. They are what black politi-

cians often like to call themselves in front of white audiences: Americans who "just happen to be black."

5   Racial innocents are individualists, perfectly happy to assimilate in an accommodating way with whites, a bargain that essentially places all obligation for racial harmony solely on blacks. They make no demands of whites except to be fair, and even then, the innocents allow the white people pretty much to determine the standard for fairness. People who "just happen to be black" may not think blacks have much that white people should trouble themselves with learning about, anyway. They may on occasion be heckled by passing carloads of young yahoos yelling racial epithets. They may on occasion suffer the indignity of being tailed in a department store or passed over by a taxicab. But they casually shrug off these offenses as "little slights," as a white person might.

6   Americans who "just happen to be black" can be perfectly happy with their lives, but they usually are young, inexperienced in the world, and ripe for a bold conversion. It usually comes after the individual has encountered racism in a way that makes the person feel constantly exposed, vulnerable to racial shame, susceptible to hurt. An accumulation of events, a series of abuses or slights by white society can be, as Lu Palmer, an African-American

activist in Chicago, likes to say, "enough to make a Negro turn Black!"

> Not all blacks see the world in the same way. And some ways of seeing it, according to Clarence Page, are more productive than others.

[7] The beginning of what some would call "true blackness," but I would call one of several versions of blackness, comes with a defensive withdrawal, a retreat into group identity and to borrow Alice Walker's marvelous phrase, the temples of the familiar. The group shelters the individual, soothes the individual's pain, and protects the individual from hurt, real or imagined. The person who had been racially neutral or even self-hating may suddenly become "Afrocentric," intellectually and emotionally centered on Africa—or, at least, on a mentally manufactured ideal of what Africa ought to be.

[8] Testing new self-images, individuals may overcompensate to prove their blackness, mostly to themselves. They may change their names to something in Swahili or Arabic, festoon themselves with new clothes, "natural" hair, flags, national colors, code phrases, party lines, ten-point programs, and blacker-than-thou ideologies.

[9] The "superblack" phase is so attractive, comfortable, and safe that some people never leave it. Group identity relieves them of such burdensome obligations as independent thinking. As Richard Hofstadter, author of *The Paranoid Style in American Politics,* might say, one no longer needs complicated explanations for a seemingly chaotic, threatening world. The paranoid view is enough. The group's joys, fears, and prejudices do quite nicely. They become one's own.

[10] The new believers are the truest believers; propelled by astonishment and guilt over their own ignorance and how much they had been blinded— duped!—by the enemies of blackness into missing its beauty, they passionately immerse themselves in all things black to make up for lost time. It is not always an easy transition. Self-consciousness over one's own discomfort can lead to even more vocal rage directed against white racism and black "Uncle Toms."

[11] "It is a paradox of social change that the most dramatic displays of the new Black image are often exhibited by those least at ease with their new identity," writes Temple University psychologist William E. Cross, Jr., in his book *Shades of Black:*

Diversity in African-American Identity (1991) which details identity changes like those described above.

[12] As blackness—"nigresence," as Cross prefers to call it—becomes a measure of one's self-esteem, every noncomformist to it becomes a direct insult, a sign of disrespect against blackness itself, and the new zealot takes it personally. Small wonder, then, that Malcolm X and other revisionist Muslims have been targeted by fellow Muslims. The heretic is always far more threatening than the complete nonbeliever.

[13] Stridency cools over time, writes Cross, and the individuals reencounter themselves. This period of reassessment is often brought on by some great disappointment or revelation. It is a crossroads. Some individuals may turn back to an earlier stage of identity development. Some may stumble instead down a path toward spiritual or mental breakdown, even suicide. A new and unpleasant eye-opener can cause other individuals to drop out of their new blackness as decidedly as they dropped in. Many gravitate to pragmatic, grass-roots, results-oriented approaches to black issues—mentoring groups, block clubs, voluntarism, or elective office, for example.

[14] They may regress to their earlier stage of "just happening to be black" or, embittered by their experience, experience a new, better-informed self-hatred. Or they may become so embittered by white society that they fixate in *hyperblackness,* the highest state of black rage, locking on to extreme anti-white attitudes and bitter nihilism. They can become the casualties of racism, the walking wounded who drop out disenchanted, or they can bottom out and turn up a new path to self-awareness and stability in which the individual transcends race. Instead of embracing race as the central focus of life, a security blanket, they use it instead as a platform, a base of operations from which they can venture forth to deal more effectively with the larger world.

[15] I think this transcendent stage marks the mind's true liberation, an exhilarating leap away from spiritual weakness to true independent strength. Malcolm X offered an excellent example when he returned from Mecca after his break with the pseudo-scientific Islam of the Honorable Elijah Muhammad. Though he was still committed to black people, his vision had expanded to that of the true *transracial man,* for whom blackness was not an end, but a beginning, his point of departure in opening himself to the larger world of ideas, cul-

tures, and experiences. Only then had he tran-
scended his own vulnerabilities, after a lifetime of
racial hurt, enough to open the door to white people in his Pan-African movement. If they were willing to assist the struggle of blacks, they were
welcome, he said. But he would not let them lead.
Some wags might have heard lasting prejudice in
this, but, in light of other ethnic struggles, it made
perfect sense. The international black liberation
movement could no more reasonably be led by

whites than the St. Patrick's Day parade could be
led by blacks.

Starting Time [   ]

Reading Time [   ]

Finishing Time [   ]

■ Reading Rate [   ]

COMPREHENSION —

Read the following questions and statements. For each one, put an X in the box before
the option that contains the most complete or accurate answer.

1. The writer quoted at the beginning of this
   selection is
   ☐ a. Zora Neale Hurston.
   ☐ b. Malcolm X.
   ☐ c. Shelby Steele.
   ☐ d. Alice Walker.

2. Clarence Page believes that blacks
   ☐ a. are generally vulnerable.
   ☐ b. are usually victims.
   ☐ c. tend to be sad and unfulfilled.
   ☐ d. can be characterized in many ways.

3. This selection is organized as
   ☐ a. a presentation of an effect, followed by
      several causes for it.
   ☐ b. a straightforward narrative telling a simple
      story.
   ☐ c. explanations and examples of various
      categories.
   ☐ d. a spatial description.

4. Page sees the development of black self-
   understanding as
   ☐ a. something that happens all at once.
   ☐ b. at its high point when a person becomes
      "Afrocentric."
   ☐ c. similar to what the Irish feel on St. Patrick's
      Day.
   ☐ d. a gradual path, with various choices along
      the way.

5. A racial innocent would
   ☐ a. choose Afrocentric clothing.
   ☐ b. express rage when a taxicab does not stop
      for him or her.
   ☐ c. not mind occasional discriminatory acts from
      whites.
   ☐ d. feel constantly exposed to racial insults.

6. Racial innocents are usually young people because
   ☐ a. young people often pay close attention to
      the world around them.
   ☐ b. as people grow older, they are more likely to
      have experienced serious discrimination.
   ☐ c. young people hate discrimination more than
      older people.
   ☐ d. racial innocence is what is taught in the
      schools nowadays.

7. Feeling "superblack" is
   ☐ a. what all blacks should work toward.
   ☐ b. a phase blacks should try to get beyond.
   ☐ c. a good way to avoid discrimination.
   ☐ d. a way for most black entertainers to feel
      comfortable.

8. The tone of paragraphs 9 and 10 is
   ☐ a. intensely angry.
   ☐ b. quite humorous.
   ☐ c. very bitter.
   ☐ d. somewhat sarcastic.

9. Malcolm X is held up as a model because he
   - ☐ a. got beyond racism to the larger world of ideas and experiences.
   - ☐ b. broke with Elijah Muhammed.
   - ☐ c. thought of himself as a black man first and foremost.
   - ☐ d. would not let whites lead his movement.

10. The last sentence of this selection makes use of
    - ☐ a. an analogy.
    - ☐ b. a simile.
    - ☐ c. a symbol.
    - ☐ d. a metaphor.

Comprehension Skills

1. recalling specific facts
2. retaining concepts
3. organizing facts
4. understanding the main idea
5. drawing a conclusion
6. making a judgment
7. making an inference
8. recognizing tone
9. understanding characters
10. appreciating literary forms

VOCABULARY, PART TWO—

Write the term that makes the most sense in each sentence.

chaotic   **zealot**
heretic   **stridency**
gravitate

1. Page believes that, depending on what attracts them, people _____ toward different degrees of blackness.

2. They do this because they are trying to bring order to a _____ world.

3. One person might become a _____, expressing very strong beliefs in the value of African ideals.

4. This sort of person sometimes shows a _____ in his or her behavior that irritates others.

5. Another person might be a _____ who no longer believes in all the ideals of Afrocentrism.

pragmatic   **regress**
transcends   **susceptible**
paradox

6. The more _____ a person is, the more likely he or she will be affected by different movements or beliefs.

7. One _____ that Page has noted is that the most dramatic displays of a black "image" come from people who are least comfortable with that image.

8. Sometimes people move forward toward more realistic beliefs, but sometimes they _____.

9. A _____ attitude is better than one that has little connection with reality.

10. The best attitude of all _____ being black and goes on to the larger world of ideas.

Comprehension Score [ ]

Vocabulary Score [ ]

WRITING—

Do you agree with Page's ideas about "superblacks"? Why or why not? Write a few paragraphs that express your thoughts on the subject. If you can, use examples from real life to back up what you say.

STUDY SKILLS —

Read the following passage and answer the questions that follow it.

Reviewing for Examinations, III

2. Develop a New Approach. This can be a technique of real value to you. Rehashing the same old stuff is not very exciting and certainly nothing to look forward to. Try approaching the subject differently; get a fresh outlook on the material.

For example, put yourself in the role of an instructor. Imagine that next semester you will be teaching this subject and you want to review it now so you'll know it well enough to teach.

For biology, take the point of view of a doctor. What does science mean to him or her? How could it be used in an actual medical practice?

Use your imagination. Be both quizmaster and contestant. Ask yourself questions aloud, and answer them aloud for a "prize" of a million dollars and a trip to Tahiti.

However you do it, adopt a fresh point of view and make the material you are studying come alive.

3. Outline the Course. This may appear to be an enormous task to undertake at the end of a semester, but it need not be. Keep your outline brief; do not exceed three pages. The thinking that goes into outlining makes for excellent reviewing.

When you have completed your outline, you will have a picture of your knowledge of the subject. Your study assignment is now organized for you. Each night attack a new part of the outline and fill in the gaps.

Actually, this technique combines two steps in one. When outlining, you are forced to deal with principles and generalizations. All of your study should be to this end: an understanding and retention of main points and principles.

You know from your own experience that you cannot recall everything about a subject. You must become selective and choose only its most important elements. As you do this, you'll be pleased to observe how the recall of major points triggers the recall of accompanying details. You'll find yourself remembering much more than you had originally thought possible.

1. Using a new _____ is a valuable learning technique.

2. Use your _____ and adopt a fresh point of view.

3. For example, to remember Clarence Page's various ways to be _____, you could try to think of people you know who characterize each of those ways.

4. It is also important to make a brief _____ of the course when you study.

5. All of your study should be aimed at understanding and retaining the _____ points and principles.

The Origin and Growth of Afro-American Literature, I

John Henrik Clarke

AUTHOR NOTES—
John Henrik Clarke was born in Union Springs, Alabama, in 1915. A graduate of New York University, he was the first teacher of African American history to be licensed in New York State. Clarke also studied at the University of Ibadan in Nigeria and the University of Ghana and has written for both the *Pittsburgh Courier* and the *Ghana Evening News*. Perhaps as a result of his experiences, Clarke has long been a strong believer that blacks should study their African heritage. He created the "Black Heritage" history series for CBS, and has won several awards for other television work.

VOCABULARY, PART ONE—
All of these terms are in the story you are about to read. Study each term and its meaning. Then answer the questions below.

As you read the story, notice how each vocabulary term is used. You will have more questions about the terms later.

misconception, an incorrect thought or idea

strife, struggle; battle

yielded, gave in; surrendered

sojourns, brief stays or visits

erudition, learnedness obtained from study

expatriation, the act of leaving one's country

attainments, achievements

conventions, customs

turbulent, disorderly; violent

stigma, mark of disgrace

1. Which word could be used in talking about short, overnight trips to a vacation spot? _____

2. Which word could identify a situation characterized by people disagreeing and arguing? _____

3. Which word names what the professors in any good school should be known for?

   _____

4. Which word tells what a bank robber did when he allowed himself to be taken prisoner? _____

5. Which word could be a synonym for *accomplishments*?

   _____

A READING PURPOSE—

This selection describes the earliest history of black scholarship and learning. As you read, notice some of the scholars that Clarke finds particularly impressive.

---

1 Africans were great story tellers long before their first appearance in Jamestown, Virginia, in 1619. The rich and colorful history, art and folklore of West Africa, the ancestral home of most Afro-Americans, present evidence of this, and more.

2 Contrary to a <u>misconception</u> which still prevails, the Africans were familiar with literature and art for many years before their contact with the Western world. Before the breaking up of the social structure of the West African states of Ghana, Melle (Mali) and Songhay, and the internal <u>strife</u> and chaos that made the slave trade possible, the forefathers of the Africans who eventually became slaves in the United States lived in a society where university life was fairly common and scholars were beheld with reverence.

3 There were in this ancestry rulers who expanded their kingdoms into empires, great and magnificent armies whose physical dimensions dwarfed entire nations into submission, generals who advanced the technique of military science, scholars whose vision of life showed foresight and wisdom, and priests who told of gods that were strong and kind. To understand fully any aspect of Afro-American life, one must realize that the black American is not without a cultural past, though he was many generations removed from it before his achievements in American literature and art commanded any appreciable attention.

4 I have been referring to the African Origin of Afro-American Literature and history. This preface is essential to every meaningful discussion of the role of the Afro-American in every major aspect of American life, past and present. Before getting into the main body of this talk I want to make it clear that the Black Race did not come to the United States culturally empty-handed.

5 I will elaborate very briefly on my statement to the effect that "the forefathers of the Africans who eventually became slaves in the United States once lived in a society where university life was fairly common and scholars were beheld with reverence."

6 During the period in West African history—from the early part of the fourteenth century to the time of the Moorish invasion in 1591, the City of Timbuktu, with the University of Sankore in the Songhay Empire, was the intellectual center of Africa. Black scholars were enjoying a renaissance that was known and respected throughout most of Africa and in parts of Europe. At this period in African history, the University of Sankore, at Timbuktu, was the educational capital of the Western Sudan. In his book *Timbuktu the Mysterious*, Felix DuBois gives us the following description of this period:

7 The scholars of Timbuktu <u>yielded</u> in nothing to the saints in their <u>sojourns</u> in the foreign univer-

sities of Fez, Tunis and Cairo. They astounded the most learned men of Islam by their <u>erudition</u>. That these Negroes were on a level with the Arabian Savants is proved by the fact that they were installed as professors in Morocco and Egypt. In contrast to this, we find that the Arabs were not always equal to the requirements of Sankore.

8 I will speak of only one of the great black scholars referred to in the book by Felix DuBois.

9 Ahmed Baba was the last chancellor of the University of Sankore. He was one of the greatest African scholars of the late sixteenth century. His life is a brilliant example of the range and depth of West African intellectual activity before the colonial era. Ahmed Baba was the author of more than 40 books: nearly every one of these books had a different theme. He was in Timbuktu when it was invaded by the Moroccans in 1592, and he was one of the first citizens to protest this occupation of his beloved home town. Ahmed Baba, along with other scholars, was imprisoned and eventually exiled to Morocco. During his <u>expatriation</u> from Timbuktu, his collection of 1,600 books, one of the richest libraries of his day, was lost.

10 Now, West Africa entered a sad period of decline. During the Moorish occupation, wreck and ruin became the order of the day. When the Europeans arrived in this part of Africa and saw these conditions, they assumed that nothing of order and value had ever existed in these countries. This mistaken impression, too often repeated, has influenced the interpretation of African and Afro-American life in history for over 400 years.

11 Negroes played an important part in American life, history and culture long before 1619. Our relationship to this country is as old as the country itself.

12 Africans first came to the new world as explorers. They participated in the exploratory expeditions of Balboa, the discoverer of the Pacific, and Cortes, the conqueror of Mexico. An African explorer helped to open up New Mexico and Arizona and prepared the way for the settlement of the Southwest. Africans also accompanied French Jesuit missionaries on their early travels through North America.

13 In the United States, the art and literature of the Negro people has had an economic origin. Much that is original in black American folklore, or singular in "Negro spirituals" and blues, can be traced to the economic institution of slavery and its influence upon the Negro's soul.

14 After the initial poetical debut of Jupiter Hammon and Phillis Wheatley, the main literary expression of the Negro was the slave narrative. One of the earliest of these narratives came from the pen of Gustavas Vassa, an African from Nigeria. This was a time of great pamphleteering in the United States. The free Africans in the North, and those who had escaped from slavery in the South, made their mark upon this time and awakened the conscience of the nation. Their lack of formal educational <u>attainments</u> gave their narratives a strong and rough-hewed truth, more arresting than scholarship.

15 Gustavas Vassa established his reputation with an autobiography, first printed in England. Vassa, born in 1745, was kidnapped by slavers when he was 11 years old and taken to America. He was placed in service on a plantation in Virginia. Eventually, he was able to purchase his freedom. He left the United States, made his home in England and became active in the British anti-slavery movement. In 1790, he presented a petition to Parliament to abolish the slave trade. His autobiography, *The Interesting Narrative of the Life of Gustavas Vassa,* was an immediate success and had to be published in five editions.

16 At the time when slave ships were still transporting Africans to the New World, two 18th century Negroes were writing and publishing works of poetry. The first of these was Jupiter Hammon, a slave in Queens Village, Long Island. In 1760, Hammon published *An Evening Thought: Salvation by Christ, With Penitential Cries....* In all probability this was the first poem published by an American Negro. His most remarkable work, "An address to the Negroes of New York," was published in 1787. Jupiter Hammon died in 1800.

17 Phillis Wheatley (1753–1784), like Hammon, was influenced by the religious forces of Wesley-Whitefield revival. Unlike Hammon, however, she was a writer of unusual talent. Though born in Africa, she acquired in an incredibly short time both the literary culture and the religion of her New England masters. Her writings reflect little of her race and much of the age in which she lived. She was a New England poet of the third quarter of the 18th century, and her poems reflected the poetic <u>conventions</u> of the Boston Puritans with whom she lived. Her fame continued long after her death in 1784 and she became one of the best known poets of New England.

18 Another important body of literature came out of this period. It is the literature of petition, written by free black men in the North, who were free in

name only. Some of the early petitioners for justice were Caribbean-Americans who saw their plight and the plight of the Afro-Americans as one and the same.

> For those who think that black history begins with slaves in America, John Henrik Clarke offers a glimpse of a great and dignified African culture.

19 In 18th century America, two of the most outstanding fighters for liberty and justice were the West Indians—Prince Hall and John B. Russwurm. When Prince Hall came to the United States, the nation was in turmoil. The colonies were ablaze with indignation. Britain, with a series of revenue acts, had stoked the fires of colonial discontent. In Virginia, Patrick Henry was speaking of liberty or death. The cry, "No Taxation Without Representation," played on the nerve strings of the nation. Prince Hall, then a delicate-looking teenager, often walked through the turbulent streets of Boston, an observer unobserved.

20 A few months before these hectic scenes, he had arrived in the United States from his home in Barbados, where he was born about 1748, the son of an Englishman and a free African woman. He was, in theory, a free man, but he knew that neither in Boston nor in Barbados were persons of African descent free in fact. At once, he questioned the sin-

cerity of the vocal white patriots of Boston. It never seemed to have occurred to them that the announced principles motivating their action was stronger argument in favor of destroying the system of slavery. The colonists held in servitude more than a half million human beings, some of them white; yet they engaged in the contradiction of going to war to support the theory that all men were created equal.

21 When Prince Hall arrived in Boston, that city was the center of the American slave trade. Most of the major leaders of revolutionary movement, in fact, were slaveholders or investors in slave-supported businesses. Hall, like many other Americans, wondered: what did these men mean by freedom?

22 The condition of the free black men, as Prince Hall found them, was not an enviable one. Emancipation brought neither freedom nor relief from the stigma of color. They were still included with slaves, indentured servants, and Indians in the slave codes. Discriminatory laws severely circumscribed their freedom of movement.

Starting Time	
Reading Time	
Finishing Time	
■ Reading Rate	

COMPREHENSION —

Read the following questions and statements. For each one, put an X in the box before the option that contains the most complete or accurate answer.

1. Which of the following cities was once the greatest intellectual center of Africa?
   □ a. Tunis
   □ b. Cairo
   □ c. Timbuktu
   □ d. Fez

2. The writer of the selection points out that
   □ a. the forefathers of today's Afro-Americans valued education.
   □ b. Europeans brought Christianity to the African continent.
   □ c. the American black was the true creator of the short story.
   □ d. initially, black people came willingly to America.

3. The facts in the selection are for the most part arranged in a type of
   - ☐ a. time order.
   - ☐ b. spatial order.
   - ☐ c. ascending order.
   - ☐ d. descending order.

4. Which of the following titles states the main idea of this passage?
   - ☐ a. The Downfall of the West African Empire
   - ☐ b. Negro Involvement in American Politics
   - ☐ c. Literacy Among Black Americans
   - ☐ d. Black Scholarship, from Africa to Colonial America

5. We can conclude from this article that black people
   - ☐ a. became involved in American politics around the 1700s.
   - ☐ b. had an important but not well-known role in America's literary past.
   - ☐ c. were often taught to read and write at an early age.
   - ☐ d. were once used as slaves in England.

6. From the facts presented in this passage, we can make the judgment that
   - ☐ a. Prince Hall was an accomplished playwright.
   - ☐ b. Gustavus Vassa was educated in England.
   - ☐ c. Phillis Wheatley was a better writer than Jupiter Hammon.
   - ☐ d. the West Indies were the birthplace of many black writers.

7. This author infers that slave trade to America was brought about by
   - ☐ a. famine in Africa.
   - ☐ b. political unrest in Africa.
   - ☐ c. the migration of black Africans.
   - ☐ d. European interference in Africa.

8. The tone of this passage is one of
   - ☐ a. grief.
   - ☐ b. indifference.
   - ☐ c. uncertainty.
   - ☐ d. pride.

9. The writers mentioned in this article probably felt that
   - ☐ a. there should be an eye for an eye.
   - ☐ b. it was important to express oneself through writing.
   - ☐ c. honesty and honor prevailed over corruption.
   - ☐ d. black people were the masters of their own ships.

10. The author uses the phrase "an observer unobserved" to say that Prince Hall was
    - ☐ a. accepted.
    - ☐ b. tolerated.
    - ☐ c. ignored.
    - ☐ d. despised.

Comprehension Skills

1. recalling specific facts
2. retaining concepts
3. organizing facts
4. understanding the main idea
5. drawing a conclusion
6. making a judgment
7. making an inference
8. recognizing tone
9. understanding characters
10. appreciating literary forms

VOCABULARY, PART TWO—

Write the term that makes the most sense in each sentence.

misconception	sojourns
erudition	attainments
stigma	

1. Many people don't know much about black history and have the _____ that it has little richness.

2. They are not aware of the many _____ of black African scholars and thinkers.

3. Because these scholars read and studied constantly, their _____ was great.

4. Many would go on _____ to other locations to learn more.

5. In fact, in some communities there was a(n) _____ attached to not taking studies seriously.

conventions   **strife**
yielded   **expatriation**
turbulent

6.   After long years of peace,

_____ finally overtook these

countries.

7.   There were _____ times when

everything orderly seemed to be destroyed.

8.   All of the customs and _____

that people had lived by were totally changed.

9.   The natives were finally overcome and

_____ to their enemies.

10. Some could not tolerate the changes in their coun-

try and preferred _____.

Comprehension Score   [   ]

Vocabulary Score   [   ]

W R I T I N G —

Many world history books have ignored the important black civilization of which Timbuktu was the center. Why do you think this is so? Write a few paragraphs expressing your opinion on the reasons for this omission.

S T U D Y   S K I L L S —

Read the following passage and answer the questions that follow it.

Reviewing for Examinations, IV

4. Know What to Expect. There is a great deal you can learn about an examination beforehand. If you are "examwise," you can plan the best way to study and the kinds of answers to prepare.

First, discover the kind of exam to be given. Essay exams require you to organize and compose your own answers. Objective tests require you to select the best response to multiple-choice questions, or to label statements true or false, or to fill in or match items. The best way to study for both types of examinations will be covered in the Study Skills of later selections.

Most instructors don't mind discussing upcoming exams in a general way. Others are very specific in advising you what to prepare for. By all means, be in class and be alert when a coming exam is being discussed.

It may also be possible to talk to those who have already taken the course to discover what sort of tests the instructor gives. Do the exams generally focus on facts and details? Do they require you to demonstrate an understanding of principles? Will you be expected to reason, to apply knowledge to a specific case? The answers to these questions require a suitable kind of study on your part.

Does the instructor have a favorite question? Is there one item that appears again and again on the tests? If so, plan your response in advance.

Don't worry yourself or your instructor trying to get advance "tips," but use wisely whatever solid information is legitimately available to you to help plan your studying.

1.   You can learn a lot about an

_____ before it is given.

2.   Find out if the examination is an essay type or if it

is an _____ type.

3.   _____ exams require you to

organize and compose your own answers.

4.   For instance, if you were to write a brief chronology

of black writers, you would have to figure out the

time _____ yourself.

5.   Always use all of the test _____

legitimately available to help you to plan your study.

The Origin and Growth of Afro-American Literature, II

John Henrik Clarke

AUTHOR NOTES—
John Henrik Clarke is well known for his work as a writer and editor. His book of poetry *Rebellion in Rhyme* followed a World War II experience as a master sergeant. Clarke co-founded the *Harlem Quarterly* and is also a co-founder of the Black Academy of Arts and Letters. Clarke's collection *A Century of Best Black American Short Stories*, of which he was general editor, was originally published in 1966 and reissued in 1993. Another work, *Africans Away from Home*, was published in 1988.

VOCABULARY, PART ONE—
All of these terms are in the story you are about to read. Study each term and its meaning. Then answer the questions below.

As you read the story, notice how each vocabulary term is used. You will have more questions about the terms later.

debased, brought to a lower value, status, or character

frugality, thrift; careful management

inherent, built-in or essential quality of something

wrath, great anger; fury

preconceived, formed or formulated in advance

cater, try to provide what is wanted

renaissance, a rebirth or reawakening

preponderance, superiority in number or extent

debunked, exposed, as in a fraud or myth

mar, spoil; damage

1. Which word identifies a quality that involves spending money carefully and trying to hold on to what one has? _____

2. Which word tells what a father might feel if his son has stolen his car and then destroyed it in a collision? _____

3. Which word tells what you do to the surface of a desk if you put a scratch in it?

   _____

4. What kind of idea would you have if you went into a movie thinking you already knew how it would end? _____

5. Which word tells what you did to a friend's excuse for cutting class if you let everyone know it was a lie? _____

A READING PURPOSE —

In this selection Clarke continues his history of black scholarship, focusing on American thinkers and writers. Read to find out more about black arts movements, such as the Harlem Renaissance.

1 By 1765, Prince Hall saw little change in the condition of the blacks, and though a freeman, at least in theory, he saw his people <u>debased</u> as though they were slaves still in bondage. These things drove him to prepare himself for leadership among his people. So, through diligence and <u>frugality</u>, he became a property owner, thus establishing himself in the eyes of white people as well as the blacks.

2 But the ownership of property was not enough. He still had to endure sneers and insults. He went to school at night, and later became a Methodist preacher. His church became the forum for his people's grievances. Ten years after his arrival in Boston, he was the accepted leader of the black community.

3 In 1788, Hall petitioned the Massachusetts Legislature, protesting the kidnapping of free Negroes. This was a time when American patriots were engaged in a constitutional struggle for freedom. They had proclaimed the <u>inherent</u> rights of all mankind to life, liberty and the pursuit of happiness. Hall dared to remind them that the black men in the United States were human beings and as such were entitled to freedom and respect for their human personality.

4 Prejudice made Hall the father of African secret societies in the United States. He is the father of what is now known as Negro Masonry. Hall first sought initiation into the white Masonic Lodge in Boston, but was turned down because of his color. He then applied to the Army Lodge of an Irish Regiment. His petition was favorably received. On March 6, 1775, Hall and fourteen other black Americans were initiated in Lodge Number 441. When, on March 17, the British were forced to evacuate Boston, the Army Lodge gave Prince Hall and his colleagues a license to meet and function as a Lodge. Thus, on July 3, 1776, African Lodge No. 1 came into being. This was the first Lodge in Masonry established in America for men of African descent.

5 The founding of the African Lodge was one of Prince Hall's greatest achievements. It afforded the Africans in the New England area a greater sense of security, and contributed to a new spirit of unity among them. Hall's interest did not end with the Lodge. He was deeply concerned with improving the lot of his people in other ways. He sought to have schools established for the children of the free Africans in Massachusetts. Of prime importance is the fact that Prince Hall worked to secure respect for the personality of his people and also played a significant role in the downfall of the Massachusetts slave trade. He helped to prepare the groundwork for the freedom fighters of the 19th and 20th centuries, whose continuing efforts have

brought the black American closer to the goal of full citizenship.

> A survey of black American writing reveals a rich, if little-known, storehouse of literary expression.

6   The literature of petition was continued by men like David Walker whose *Appeal,* an indictment of slavery, was published in 1829. Dynamic ministers like Samuel Ringgold Ward and Henry Highland Garnet joined the ranks of the petitioners at the time a journalist literature was being born.

7   Frederick Douglass, the noblest of American black men of the 19th century, was the leader of the journalist group. He established the newspaper *North Star* and, later, the magazine *Douglass Monthly*. John B. Russwurm and Samuel Cornish founded the newspaper *Freedom's Journal* in 1827.

8   In 1829, a third poet, George Moses Horton, published his book, *The Hope of Liberty*. In his second volume, *Naked Genius,* (1865), he expressed his anti-slavery convictions more clearly. George Moses Horton was the first slave poet to openly protest his status.

9   Throughout the early part of the 19th century, the slave narrative became a new form of American literary expression.

10   The best known of these slave narratives came from the pen of Frederick Douglass, the foremost Negro in the anti-slavery movement. His first book was *The Narrative of the Life of Frederick Douglass* (1845). Ten years later, an improved and enlarged edition, *My Bondage and My Freedom,* was published. His third autobiography, *Life and Times of Frederick Douglass,* was published in 1881 and enlarged in 1892. Douglass fought for civil rights and against lynching and the Ku Klux Klan. No abuse of justice escaped his attention and his <u>wrath</u>.

11   It was not until 1887 that an Afro-American writer emerged who was fully a master of the short story as a literary form. This writer was Charles W. Chesnutt. Chesnutt, an Ohioan by birth, became a teacher in North Carolina while still in his middle teens. He studied the traditions and superstitions of the people that he taught and later made this material into the ingredient of his best short stories. In August 1887, his short story "The Goophered Grapevine," appeared in the *Atlantic Monthly*. This was the beginning of a series of stories which were later brought together in his first book, *The Conjure Woman* (1899). "The Wife of His Youth" also ap-

peared in the *Atlantic* (July 1898) and gave the title to his second volume, *The Wife of His Youth and Other Stories of the Color Line* (1899). Three more stories appeared later: "Baxter's Procrustes" in the <u>Atlantic</u> (June 1904), and "The Doll" and "Mr. Taylor's Funeral" in *The Crisis* magazine (April 1912 and April–May 1915).

12   Chesnutt's novel did not measure up to the standards he had set with his short stories, though they were all competently written. In 1928, he was awarded the Spingarn Medal for his "pioneer work as a literary artist depicting the life and struggle of Americans of Negro descent."

13   Paul Laurence Dunbar, a contemporary of Charles W. Chesnutt, made his reputation as a poet before extending his talent to short stories. Both Dunbar and Chesnutt very often used the same subject matter in their stories. Chesnutt was by far the better writer, and his style and attitude differed radically from Dunbar's.

14   Dunbar's pleasant folk tales of tradition-bound plantation black folk were more acceptable to a large white reading audience with <u>preconceived</u> ideas of "Negro characteristics." In all fairness, it must be said that Dunbar did not <u>cater</u> to this audience in all of his stories. In such stories as "The Tragedy at Three Forks," "The Lynching of Jube Benson" and "The Ordeal of Mt. Hope," he showed a deep concern and understanding of the more serious and troublesome aspects of Afro-American life. Collections of his stories are: *Folks from Dixie* (1898), *The Strength of Gideon* (1900), *In Old Plantation Days* (1903), and *The Heart of Happy Hollow* (1904). Only one of his novels, *The Sport of the Gods* (1902), is mainly concerned with Afro-American characters.

15   Chesnutt and Dunbar, in their day, reached a larger general reading audience than any of the black writers who came before them. The period of the slave narratives had passed. Yet, the black writer was still an oddity and a stepchild in the eyes of most critics. This attitude continued in a lessening degree throughout one of the richest and most productive periods in Afro-American writing in the United States—the period called "the Negro <u>Renaissance</u>." The community of Harlem was the center and spiritual godfather and midwife for this renaissance. The cultural emancipation of the Afro-American that began before the first World War was now in full force. The black writer discovered a new voice within himself and liked the sound of it. The white writers who had been interpreting our life with an air of authority and a <u>preponderance</u> of

error looked at last to the black writer for their next cue. In short story collections like Jean Toomer's *Cane* (1923) and Langston Hughes' *The Ways of White Folks* (1934) heretofore untreated aspects of Afro-American life were presented in an interesting manner that was unreal to some readers because it was new and so contrary to the stereotypes they had grown accustomed to.

16 In her book *Mules and Men* (1935), Zora Neal Hurston presented a collection of folk tales and sketches that showed the close relationship between humor and tragedy in Afro-American life. In doing this, she also fulfilled the first requirement of all books—to entertain and guide the reader through an interesting experience that is worth the time and attention it takes to absorb it. In other stories like *The Gilded Six Bits, Drenched in Light,* and *Spunk* another side of Miss Hurston's talent was shown.

17 In the midst of this renaissance, two strong voices from the West Indians were heard. Claude McKay in his books *Ginger-Town* (1932) and *Banana Bottom* (1933), wrote of life in his Jamaican homeland in a manner that debunked the travelogue exoticism usually attributed to Negro life in the Caribbean area. Before the publication of these books, Harlem and its inhabitants had already been the subject matter for a group of remarkable short stories by McKay and the inspiration for his book, *Home to Harlem,* still the most famous novel ever written about that community.

18 In 1926, Eric Walrond, a native of British Guiana, explored and presented another side of West Indian life in his book, *Tropic Death,* a near classic. In these 10 naturalistic stories, Eric Walrond concerns himself mostly with labor and living conditions in the Panama Canal Zone where a diversity of people and ways of life meet and clash, while each tries to survive at the expense of the other. Clear perception and strength of style enabled Mr. Walrond to balance form and content in such a manner that the message was never intruded upon the unfolding of the stories.

19 Rudolph Fisher, another bright star of the Harlem literary renaissance, was first a brilliant young doctor. The new and light touch he brought to his stories of Afro-American life did not mar the serious aspect that was always present. The message in his comic realism was more profound because he was skillful enough to weave it into the design of his stories without destroying any of their entertainment value. His stories "Blades of Steel," "The City of Refuge" and "The Promised Land" were published in the *Atlantic Monthly*. "High Yaller" appeared in *The Crisis* magazine during the hey-day of that publication, and was later reprinted in the O'Brien anthology, *Best Short Stories of 1934*. Unfortunately, he died before all of his bright promise was fulfilled.

20 The Harlem literary renaissance was studded with many names. Those already mentioned are only a few of the most outstanding. During the period of this literary flowering among black writers, Harlem became the Mecca, the stimulating Holy City, drawing pilgrims from all over the country and from some places abroad. Talented authors, playwrights, painters and sculptors came forth eagerly showing their wares.

Starting Time

Reading Time

Finishing Time

■ Reading Rate

C O M P R E H E N S I O N —

Read the following questions and statements. For each one, put an X in the box before the option that contains the most complete or accurate answer.

1. Charles W. Chesnutt was noted for his
    ☐ a. plays.
    ☐ b. novels.
    ☐ c. poetry.
    ☐ d. short stories.

2. We can make the generalization that, in their own way, many black writers
    ☐ a. were civil rights leaders.
    ☐ b. wrote to please the white population.
    ☐ c. fostered religion among black people.
    ☐ d. tried to humor black people into submission.

3. The writers discussed in the selection are presented in
   ☐ a. the order of their importance.
   ☐ b. spatial order.
   ☐ c. chronological order.
   ☐ d. ascending order.

4. This selection mainly traces
   ☐ a. Afro-American religion.
   ☐ b. the rise and fall of slavery.
   ☐ c. aspects of colonial American life.
   ☐ d. the rise of black literature.

5. What part of America did Charles W. Chesnutt come from?
   ☐ a. the South
   ☐ b. the Midwest
   ☐ c. New England
   ☐ d. the West Coast

6. Prince Hall was probably accepted by both blacks and whites because he was
   ☐ a. well educated.
   ☐ b. spiritually moral.
   ☐ c. economically successful.
   ☐ d. nonviolent.

7. Eric Walrond wrote about
   ☐ a. economic conditions of the Panama Canal Zone.
   ☐ b. agriculture in Central America.
   ☐ c. religious life in Harlem.
   ☐ d. Negro life in the Caribbean area.

8. The tone of the selection is
   ☐ a. serious and straightforward.
   ☐ b. bitter and sarcastic.
   ☐ c. humorous and lighthearted.
   ☐ d. regretful and sad.

9. In some of his writings, Frederick Douglass can be characterized as
   ☐ a. sadistic.
   ☐ b. humorous.
   ☐ c. angry.
   ☐ d. relaxed.

10. The last paragraph of the article
    ☐ a. introduces a new subject.
    ☐ b. changes the setting.
    ☐ c. presents a problem.
    ☐ d. serves as a summary.

Comprehension Skills

1. recalling specific facts
2. retaining concepts
3. organizing facts
4. understanding the main idea
5. drawing a conclusion
6. making a judgment
7. making an inference
8. recognizing tone
9. understanding characters
10. appreciating literary forms

VOCABULARY, PART TWO —

Write the term that makes the most sense in each sentence.

frugality   **inherent**
cater   **renaissance**
preponderance

1. A great rebirth of black literature began during the Harlem _____ in the 1920s.

2. During that time, as today, a great _____ of Harlem's population, far more than half, was black.

3. Not everyone there had a great deal of money; most practiced _____ to make ends meet.

4. The bars and nightclubs in the area were proud of their black customers and tried to _____ to their every need.

5. The _____ belief of most Harlem residents was that this was a time of great promise.

wrath   **debased**
preconceived   **mar**
debunked

6. Whites who ventured into Harlem thought they knew what to expect: they had _____ notions of what conditions were like.

7. Their views of blacks as merely happy-go-lucky performers _____ the value of the black race.

8. The whites' ideas were usually _____ when they saw that life in Harlem actually had much variety.

9. Some whites got angry and expressed their _____ that things in Harlem were not as they had thought.

10. They did not want the cold light of reality to _____ their wishful ideas.

Comprehension Score [ ]

Vocabulary Score [ ]

WRITING —
Harlem was the bustling, crowded section of New York where much black literary and theatrical development took place. Would you have liked to live in Harlem during its reawakening period? Why or why not? Write a few paragraphs explaining your feelings.

STUDY SKILLS —
Read the following passage and answer the questions that follow it.

Reviewing for Examinations, V
5. Study Quizzes. Study the other tests and quizzes you have taken during the term. Some of the same questions, or variations of them, might be asked again.

All teachers stress what they consider important on quizzes during the term. Reviewing past tests will assure that you will be covering many of the most important topics in the course.

6. Review Class Questions. Like the rest of us, teachers are creatures of habit. They tend to repeat them-

selves. During the term, make notes on the questions your instructor asked in class. You can feel confident that questions like these will appear again.

Be sure to copy down accurately everything mentioned by the instructor in the pre-exam review. Many lecturers devote their final class to summarizing the course. Questions asked at this time are particularly significant because the instructor is speaking with the exam in mind.

7. Cram. Devote the final night to cramming. Spend your last moments in an intensive review of all major facts, principles, and generalizations. Do not be concerned with details at this time; they'll come back to you later.

Cover the items on your outline fully. Be sure that you can define, explain, or describe what is important or essential to each major point.

8. Be Ready. Do not stay up too late the night before. Staying up may create worry and anxiety—just the situation you want to avoid in the morning.

On the day of the exam, get up early and have breakfast. Even if it is not your custom to eat, have something. Nervousness can bring on distracting hunger pangs.

Have confidence in your ability. Follow the procedures suggested here, and you'll give a good performance. The best cure for exam jitters is preparation.

1. Some _____ from old examinations may be asked again.

2. Questions asked by the professor in _____ will probably appear of the test.

3. Instructors speak during their pre-exam _____ with the test in mind.

4. An intensive review of all major facts is called _____.

5. Such a review of Clarke's history of black writers would focus on major generalizations rather than _____.

18 A Century of Negro Portraiture in American Literature

Sterling A. Brown

AUTHOR NOTES—

Sterling Brown was a poet, literary critic, and teacher who was born in Washington, D.C., in 1901. After receiving a master's degree from Harvard in 1924 he taught at a number of universities, but spent the most years at Howard, where his father had also been a professor.

Brown's first volume of poetry, *Southern Road,* was published in 1932; other collections followed. Most of his poems deal with real-life situations of blacks, particularly their endurance in the face of hardship. Brown also wrote many books and articles involved with the study of African American literature, folklore, and music; he was one of the first to systematically study these areas. He died in 1989.

VOCABULARY, PART ONE—

All of these terms are in the story you are about to read. Study each term and its meaning. Then answer the questions below.

As you read the story, notice how each vocabulary term is used. You will have more questions about the terms later.

frailty, physical or emotional weakness

canniness, shrewdness; cleverness

oblique, indirect; not to the point

irrepressible, something that cannot be repressed or restrained

pertinent, relevant; necessary to the matter at hand

minute, very small

tentative, hesitating; uncertain

maladjusted, poorly adjusted

disillusioned, disappointed; rid of any expectations

compensate, make up for

1. Which word could describe a child who doesn't seem ready for school and can't get along with his classmates? _____

2. Which word tells how a person might feel if she were promised three jobs and then didn't get any of them? _____

3. Which word could describe an extremely tiny portion of something?

   _____

4. Which word could identify the condition of an elderly person who can walk only a few steps without stopping to rest? _____

5. Which word could describe an agreement that all the participants feel they may later change their minds about? _____

A READING PURPOSE —

This selection tells of the way various whites, beginning with the author of *Uncle Tom's Cabin*, wrote about blacks in the 19th century. Read to learn about the different views of blacks that they presented.

1   Over a century ago, in November, 1863, Harriet Beecher Stowe wrote that she was going to Washington to satisfy herself that "the Emancipation Proclamation was a reality and a substance not to fizzle out...." She meant to talk to "Father Abraham himself." When she was ushered into his study, her <u>frailty</u> startled President Lincoln. As his big knotted hand took her small one, he quizzed: "So this is the little lady who made this big war." Pressed by her eagerness, Lincoln assured Harriet Beecher Stowe that he was determined to issue the Emancipation Proclamation on New Year's Day.

2   In spite of Lincoln's gallant exaggeration, his estimate of the impact of *Uncle Tom's Cabin* showed his old <u>canniness</u>. His secretary of state, not so given to overstatement, said that "without *Uncle Tom's Cabin* there would have been no Abraham Lincoln"; and here William Seward also spoke cannily. For the novel had been an instantaneous success here and abroad. Many of Father Abraham's hundred thousand strong had read it a decade earlier in their forming years; many carried it in their knapsacks, and it had dramatized for both North and South the American moral dilemmas and something of the humanity involved in the controversy over slavery.

3   Herman Melville had expressed antislavery opinions even earlier in *Mardi*. The approach, however, was <u>oblique</u>, and the antislavery sections were only a

■ small part of a murky allegory, which was to be largely unread in contrast to Mrs. Stowe's popular success. Still, *Mardi* is <u>pertinent</u> here for Melville's clear indictment of slavery, his dread and prophecy of the inevitable clash of the irreconcilable viewpoints about slavery and the Negro. Describing the Capitol of Vivenza (his name for the United States) Melville singled out the creed "All Men are born Free and Equal," noting that an addition, in <u>minute</u> hieroglyphics, read: "all except the tribe of Hamo." On the flag being hoisted over the Capitol, red stripes corresponded to marks on the back of the slave who was doing the hoisting. Strangers visiting the South of Vivenza discovered that the slaves were men. For this a haughty spokesman denounced them as "firebrands come to light the flame of revolt." This grim prophet, a fictionalized Calhoun properly named Nullo, swore that the first blow struck for the slaves would "dissolve the Union of Vivenza's vales." Like his allegorical visitors, Melville was troubled over what seemed an <u>irrepressible</u> conflict between North and South and, dreading war, concluded that only Time "must befriend these thralls." In spite of his doubts about the best course, he was nevertheless certain that slavery was "a blot, foul as the crater pool of hell."

4   These two significant novelists of a century ago indicate how influential the treatment of Negro life

and character has been in American history and litera- ture. From the out- set of our national life "Negro charac- ter," if such a loose term may be used at the beginning of this essay, has in- trigued American authors. Their por- traits have evinced

> Before black people could be accurately represented in literature, the obstacles of vagueness, stereotyping, and untruth had to be overcome.

varying degrees of sympathy and understanding, skill and power. Their motives have been manifold. Their success has not been marked.

5 Before the Civil War creative literature dealing with Negro life was abundant, though not distinguished. Minor efforts at real characterizations—some per- ceptive, some vague, some tentative guesses about half-strangers—occur in Cooper, Poe, William Gilmore Simms, and the southern humorists. By and large, however, the Negro in the literature of this period was a mere pawn in the growing debate over slavery. With the overwhelming success of *Uncle Tom's Cabin* in 1852 the battle of the books was joined, and torrents of proslavery replies rushed from the presses. These were ungainly books, crude sentimentalizings and melodramatizings of the proslavery argument of Dew and Harper, of Calhoun and Fitzhugh. Slaves chanted paeans to the Arcadi- an existence of the old South; others walked the woods as embodiments of the various Bible Defenses of Slavery—one of them, for instance, pulling a much thumbed copy of the Sacred Book out of his overalls to confound a Yankee abolitionist who was haunting this Eden. The wisest slaves rejected free- dom; the maladjusted and the half-wits ran away to the North where they either died in snow drifts (they needed master to tell them to come in out of the snow) or else they saw the light, and stole away, back to the Southland and slavery (a kind of Underground Railroad in reverse). One novel, *Life at the South, or Uncle Tom's Cabin As It Is* closes with another Tom, disillusioned with the North, heading back South. "And if the reader shall chance to trav-

el the high road, as it winds up the valley of the Shenandoah, above Winchester, he will find no slave more contented than Uncle Tom." A tall, tall order. Carry me back to old Virginny.

6 They would have to carry him back to get him there, was what a Negro like Frederick Douglass thought; and this opinion was shared by such other stout-hearted fugitives as Martin Delany, David Rug- gles, Sojourner Truth, Harriet Tubman, and William Wells Brown. These and many other Negroes fought in the antislavery crusade; several used stirring au- tobiographies, pamphlets, journalism and oratory in the battle. Creative literature, however, was the ex- ception with them; an embattled people used litera- ture as a weapon, as propaganda; not as exploration, but as exposé of injustice. There were a few short stories and novels, and hortatory poetry. The truth of Negro life and character, however, is in such an autobiography as Douglass's *My Bondage and My Freedom* more than in the fiction and poetry of the time.

7 Also engaged in this crusade were white abolitionist poets—Byrant, Longfellow, Whittier—and novelists like Harriet Beecher Stowe. Their hearts were better than their circumstantial material; they, as Lowell said of Mrs. Stowe, "instinctively went right to the organic elements of human nature, whether under a white skin or black"; they knew the right thing— that men should be free. But they lacked realistic knowledge of Negro life and experience, and for this lack sentimental idealism could not compensate. Before the Civil War, therefore, the characterization of the Negro was far from the complexity that we now know was there; it was oversimplified—the contented slave, and his corollary, the wretched freedman; the comic minstrel on the one hand, and the persecuted victim, the noble savage, the sub- missive Christian, the tragic octoroon on the other.

Starting Time

Reading Time

Finishing Time

Reading Rate

COMPREHENSION —

Read the following questions and statements. For each one, put an X in the box before the option that contains the most complete or accurate answer.

1. Who wrote *Mardi*?
   - ☐ a. Harriet Beecher Stowe
   - ☐ b. Herman Melville
   - ☐ c. William Gilmore Simms
   - ☐ d. Martin Delany

2. Before the Civil War, literature of black life was
   - ☐ a. abundant but not always realistic.
   - ☐ b. factual and accurate.
   - ☐ c. mostly biographical.
   - ☐ d. graphic and discouraging.

3. The facts presented in paragraphs 4 and 5 use a type of
   - ☐ a. ascending order.
   - ☐ b. spatial development.
   - ☐ c. order of importance.
   - ☐ d. comparison and contrast.

4. This selection mainly tells us that around the time of the Civil War,
   - ☐ a. black people's lives and characters were oversimplified in the literature of the time.
   - ☐ b. black authors gave arousing accounts of black suffering and pain.
   - ☐ c. literature of the period accurately reflected the conflict and turmoil of the nation.
   - ☐ d. there was a revival of black literature, music, and art.

5. Paragraph 2 of this article leads us to conclude that *Uncle Tom's Cabin* was
   - ☐ a. a dull depiction of slave life.
   - ☐ b. sarcastic.
   - ☐ c. shallow and irrelevant.
   - ☐ d. popular worldwide.

6. We can make the judgment that pro-slavery authors often
   - ☐ a. treated the Negro with dignity and respect.
   - ☐ b. presented their arguments in a highly emotional manner.
   - ☐ c. were critical of the white establishment.
   - ☐ d. put forth sound and valid arguments for their cause.

7. We can infer from this article that Melville
   - ☐ a. was a well-educated author.
   - ☐ b. offered no solution to solve the problem of slavery.
   - ☐ c. saw the white establishment as a type of safeguard.
   - ☐ d. condemned the slave for his apathetic spirit.

8. The tone of this passage is
   - ☐ a. humorous.
   - ☐ b. hopeful.
   - ☐ c. respectful.
   - ☐ d. serious.

9. The first paragraph reveals that Harriet Beecher Stowe was
   - ☐ a. creative.
   - ☐ b. honest.
   - ☐ c. determined.
   - ☐ d. bitter.

10. When the author says, "they needed master to tell them to come in out of the snow," he is being
    - ☐ a. sarcastic.
    - ☐ b. redundant.
    - ☐ c. defensive.
    - ☐ d. truthful.

Comprehension Skills

1. recalling specific facts
2. retaining concepts
3. organizing facts
4. understanding the main idea
5. drawing a conclusion
6. making a judgment
7. making an inference
8. recognizing tone
9. understanding characters
10. appreciating literary forms

VOCABULARY, PART TWO —

Write the term that makes the most sense in each sentence.

frailty   canniness
minute   maladjusted
compensate

1. Writers who favored slavery showed blacks who escaped from it as _____, unable to find their place in life.

2. They were shown as having _____ amounts of intelligence and even less common sense.

3. Far from possessing any _____, they were portrayed as too foolish to be able to cope with the free world.

4. Between the inexperience of the young and the _____ of the old, they made poor free citizens.

5. Their determination to be free could not _____ for their other short-comings.

tentative   oblique
irrepressible   pertinent
disillusioned

6. People who wanted the slaves to be free were often disappointed and _____ when they read some of these pro-slavery novels.

7. They knew that many blacks had a(n) _____ spirit that carried them through even very difficult times.

8. They were not the hesitant, _____ people these novels made them out to be.

9. One fact that discredited these novels was that they were not subtle or _____, but instead quite exaggerated in their portrayals.

10. Pointing up these foolish exaggerations seemed a _____ way for critics to show the books' weaknesses.

Comprehension Score ☐

Vocabulary Score ☐

WRITING —

Uncle Tom's Cabin had a profound effect on its readers. Think of a book you've read that had a similar effect on you. Write a few paragraphs describing the book and telling why it impressed you so much.

STUDY SKILLS —

Read the following passage and answer the questions that follow it.

Taking Objective Exams

Objective-type examinations consist of multiple-choice, matching, fill-in, and similar type questions. Answering questions on objective examinations will produce better results if you follow these rules and steps.

Rule 1. Answer all of the questions. Even when you are penalized for wrong answers, your chances of scoring higher are better if you follow a hunch rather than leave the question unanswered.

Rule 2. Do not change an answer unless you know for sure that it is incorrect. Sometimes, a later question may reveal that one of your earlier responses was wrong. Otherwise, go with your first choice.

Rule 3. Use all of the time. Do not be tempted to finish early. Give yourself every advantage. Take every bit of the time scheduled for the examination.

Keeping these three rules in mind, follow these procedures when you answer the questions.

ANSWER EASY QUESTIONS
Divide the examination period into three equal parts. During the first period, read all of the questions. Answer

those that are easy and that have answers you know immediately. If you must stop to think over a response, go on to the next question. Doing the easy ones first helps to settle you down. We all tend to be anxious at first, and seeing questions we know the answers to eliminates uncertainty about what to expect. Also, answering the easy ones gets us off to a secure start.

ANSWER LESS DIFFICULT QUESTIONS
During the second period, read all of the unanswered questions. If after a brief pause you can supply an answer, mark it and go on. Follow your hunches now. Mark all of those you think you know. Leave the most difficult blank.

ANSWER DIFFICULT QUESTIONS
During the third round you will have more time to spend answering the difficult questions. Take your time and choose the best or most likely answer. Answer all the questions this time.

1. Objective exams consist of

   _____, matching, and fill-in

   questions.

2. Your chances for a high score are better if you answer _____ of the questions.

3. It is wise to use all of the

   _____ provided and not be

   tempted to finish early.

4. Answer the easiest questions first, leaving the most difficult until _____.

5. For example, answer factual questions such as the

   name of the woman who was the

   _____ of *Uncle Tom's Cabin*.

19 | Lynch Law in All Its Phases

Ida B. Wells-Barnett

AUTHOR NOTES—

Ida B. Wells was born in 1862 and grew up in Holly Springs, Mississippi. Her parents died when she was a teenager, leaving her to raise her younger brothers and sisters. She went to an industrial training school set up for blacks, and eventually became a teacher in Memphis, where she had moved her family. Wells then became interested in newspaper writing and worked for *The Evening Star* in Memphis before becoming editor and part owner of the *Memphis Free Speech*. She used her various newspaper positions to speak out about lynching.

Wells went to Chicago in 1893 to criticize the racism in hiring practices at the World's Fair there. In Chicago she married journalist Ferdinand Barnett of the *Chicago Conservator* and had four children. Until her death in 1931 she continued as a crusader for black rights, helping with the formation of the National Association for the Advancement of Colored People in 1909 and giving many public speeches.

VOCABULARY, PART ONE—

All of these terms are in the story you are about to read. Study each term and its meaning. Then answer the questions below.

As you read the story, notice how each vocabulary term is used. You will have more questions about the terms later.

inclination, preference; tendency

conviction, belief

apathy, unconcern; indifference

obtains, is customary

imperiling, endangering

proscriptions, limitations; bans

harboring, giving a hiding place to

vigilance, watchfulness

provocation, something that stirs up or provokes

scoffed, ridiculed; refused to take seriously

1. Which word tells what you might be doing to yourself if you drive without seat belts? _____

2. Which word identifies the condition of a person who has no interest in anything going on around her? _____

3. Which word might be used to name rules that prevent you from making certain turns in traffic? _____

4. Which word could tell what you did if you made fun of a ghost story a friend told you? _____

5. Which word identifies the attitude of a person who constantly checks to make sure no one is breaking into her house? _____

A READING PURPOSE—

This selection describes the events leading up to and following a lynching. As you read, notice the details Ida B. Wells-Barnett uses to make the episode come alive.

1 I am before the American people to-day through no <u>inclination</u> of my own, but because of a deep-seated <u>conviction</u> that the country at large does not know the extent to which lynch law prevails in parts of the Republic, nor the conditions which force into exile those who speak the truth. I cannot believe that the <u>apathy</u> and indifference which so largely <u>obtains</u> regarding mob rule is other than the result of ignorance of the true situation. And yet, the observing and thoughtful must know that in one section, at least, of our common country, a government of the people, by the people, and for the people, means a government by the mob; where the land of the free and home of the brave means a land of lawlessness, murder and outrage; and where liberty of speech means the license of might to destroy the business and drive from home those who exercise this privilege contrary to the will of the mob. Repeated attacks on the life, liberty and happiness of any citizen or class of citizens are attacks on distinctive American institutions; such attacks <u>imperiling</u> as they do the foundation of government, law and order, merit the thoughtful consideration of far-sighted Americans; not from a standpoint of sentiment, not even so much from a standpoint of justice to a weak race, as from a desire to preserve our institutions....

2 Until this past year I was one among those who believed the condition of the masses gave large excuse for the humiliations and proscriptions under which we labored; that when wealth, education and character became more general among us,—the cause being removed—the effect would cease, and justice be accorded to all alike. I shared the general belief that good newspapers entering regularly the homes of our people in every state could do more to bring about this result than any agency. Preaching the doctrine of self-help, thrift and economy every week, they would be the teachers to those who had been deprived of school advantages, yet were making history every day—and train to think for themselves our mental children of a larger growth. And so, three years ago last June, I became editor and part owner of the *Memphis Free Speech*.... I set out to make a race newspaper pay—a thing which older and wiser heads said could not be done. But there were enough of our people in Memphis and surrounding territory to support a paper, and I believed they would do so. With nine months' hard work the circulation increased from 1,500 to 3,500; in twelve months it was on a good paying basis. Throughout the Mississippi Valley in Arkansas, Tennessee and Mississippi—on plantations and in towns, the demand for and interest in the paper increased among the masses. The newsboys who would not sell it on the trains, voluntarily testified that they had never known colored people to demand a paper so eagerly.

3   To make the paper a paying business I became advertising agent, solicitor, as well as editor, and was continually on the go. Wherever I went among the people, I gave them in church, school, public gatherings, and home, the benefit of my honest conviction that maintenance of character, money getting and education would finally solve our problem and that it depended on us to say how soon this would be brought about. This sentiment bore good fruit in Memphis. We had nice homes, representatives in almost every branch of business and profession, and refined society. We had learned that helping each other helped all, and every well-conducted business by Afro-Americans prospered. With all our proscriptions in theatres, hotels and on railroads, we had never had a lynching and did not believe we could have one. There had been lynchings and brutal outrages of all sorts in our own state and those adjoining us, but we had confidence and pride in our city and the majesty of its laws. So far in advance of other Southern cities was ours, we were content to endure the evils we had, to labor and to wait.

4   But there was a rude awakening. On the morning of March 9 [1892], the bodies of three of our best young men were found in an old field horribly shot to pieces. These young men had owned and operated the "People's Grocery," situated at what was known as the Curve—a suburb made up almost entirely of colored people—about a mile from city limits. Thomas Moss, one of the oldest letter-carriers in the city, was president of the company, Calvin McDowell was manager and Will Stewart was a clerk. There were about ten other stockholders, all colored men. The young men were well known and popular and their business flourished, and that of Barrett, a white grocer who kept store there before the "People's Grocery" was established, went down. One day an officer came to the "People's Grocery" and inquired for a colored man who lived in the neighborhood, and for whom the officer had a warrant. Barrett was with him and when McDowell said he knew nothing as to the whereabouts of the man for whom they were searching, Barrett, not the officer, then accused McDowell of harboring the man, and McDowell gave the lie. Barrett drew his pistol and struck McDowell with it; thereupon McDowell, who was a tall, fine-looking six-footer, took Barrett's pistol from him, knocked him down and gave him a good thrashing, while Will Stewart, the clerk, kept the special officer at bay. Barrett went to town, swore out a warrant for their arrest on a charge of assault and battery. McDowell went before the Crim-

> The year was 1892, almost thirty years after the Civil War. Why were blacks still not protected under the law?

inal Court, immediately gave bond and returned to his store. Barrett then threatened (to use his own words) that he was going to clean out the whole store. Knowing how anxious he was to destroy their business, these young men consulted a lawyer who told them they were justified in defending themselves if attacked, as they were a mile beyond city limits and police protection. They accordingly armed several of their friends—not to assail, but to resist the threatened Saturday night attack.

5   When they saw Barrett enter the front door and a half dozen men at the rear door at 11 o'clock that night, they supposed the attack was on and immediately fired into the crowd, wounding three men. These men, dressed in citizen's clothes, turned out to be deputies who claimed to be hunting another man for whom they had a warrant, and whom any one of them could have arrested without trouble. When these men found they had fired upon officers of the law, they threw away their firearms and submitted to arrest, confident they should establish their innocence of intent to fire upon officers of the law. The daily papers in flaming headlines roused the evil passions of the whites, denounced these poor boys in unmeasured terms, nor permitted them a word in their own defense.

6   The neighborhood of the Curve was searched next day, and about thirty persons were thrown into jail, charged with conspiracy. No communication was to be had with friends any of the three days these men were in jail; bail was refused and Thomas Moss was not allowed to eat the food his wife prepared for him. The judge is reported to have said, "Any one can see them after three days." They were seen after three days, but they were no longer able to respond to the greetings of friends. On Tuesday following the shooting at the grocery, the papers which had made much of the sufferings of the wounded deputies, and promised it would go hard with those who did the shooting, if they died, announced that the officers were all out of danger, and would recover. The friends of the prisoners breathed more easily and relaxed their vigilance. They felt that as the officers would not die, there was no danger that in the heat of passion the prisoners would meet violent death at the hands of the mob. Besides, we had such confidence in the law.

But the law did not provide capital punishment for shooting which did not kill. So the mob did what the law could not be made to do, as a lesson to the Afro-American that he must not shoot a white man,—no matter what the provocation. The same night after the announcement was made in the papers that the officers would get well, the mob, in obedience to a plan known to every prominent white man in the city, went to the jail between two and three o'clock in the morning, dragged out these young men, hatless and shoeless, put them on the yard engine of the railroad which was in waiting just behind the jail, carried them a mile north of city limits and horribly shot them to death while the locomotive at a given signal let off steam and blew the whistle to deaden the sound of the firing....

7   I have no power to describe the feeling of horror that possessed every member of the race in Memphis when the truth dawned upon us that the protection of the law which we had so long enjoyed ■ was no longer ours; all this had been destroyed in a night, and the barriers of the law had been thrown down, and the guardians of the public peace and confidence scoffed away into the shadows, and all authority given into the hands of the mob, and innocent men cut down as if they were brutes.... It was our first object lesson in the doctrine of white supremacy; an illustration of the South's cardinal principle that no matter what the attainments, character or standing of an Afro-American, the laws of the South will not protect him against a white man.

Starting Time	
Reading Time	
Finishing Time	
Reading Rate	

COMPREHENSION —

Read the following questions and statements. For each one, put an X in the box before the option that contains the most complete or accurate answer.

1. Wells-Barnett's profession was
   - ☐ a. newspaper editor.
   - ☐ b. professional speaker.
   - ☐ c. elementary school teacher.
   - ☐ d. lawyer.

2. The purpose of Wells-Barnett's speech was to
   - ☐ a. tell how young black men could succeed in business.
   - ☐ b. make the public aware of the frequent occurrence of lynchings.
   - ☐ c. explain how black-owned newspapers could benefit their readers.
   - ☐ d. show that the Civil War was still going on in some parts of the country.

3. The ideas in this selection are developed through
   - ☐ a. a series of short anecdotes designed to make a point.
   - ☐ b. two anecdotes that contrast law-abiding citizens and lawbreakers.
   - ☐ c. an introduction and a lengthy anecdote.
   - ☐ d. short biographical sketches of several prominent blacks.

4. The story of the three young men being shot is meant to show that
   - ☐ a. certain whites would take the law into their own hands to get the results they wanted.
   - ☐ b. capital punishment should have been outlawed in Tennessee.
   - ☐ c. jails should have been more sturdily constructed.
   - ☐ d. blacks were generally punished if they set themselves up in business.

5. Wells-Barnett's attitude about the black grocer "thrashing" the white grocer was that it was
   - ☐ a. an unjust action that never should have happened.
   - ☐ b. justified under the circumstances.
   - ☐ c. a mistake in judgment.
   - ☐ d. proof that the community needed better law enforcement.

6. The thing about the incident that shocked the black community most was that
   - ☐ a. the young black men were not armed when they were attacked.
   - ☐ b. the whites' only motive was to get the white grocer back in business.
   - ☐ c. the rule of law that they thought protected them had been cast aside.
   - ☐ d. there had been no black police officers to protect them.

7. Barrett, the white grocer, went after the black store owner because he
   - ☐ a. was jealous of the black man's success.
   - ☐ b. wanted to steal certain merchandise from the black man's store.
   - ☐ c. wanted to prove that the black store owner had a bad temper.
   - ☐ d. wanted to see that the law was enforced in the black community.

8. Wells-Barnett's tone throughout this selection is one of
   - ☐ a. sadness.
   - ☐ b. calm.
   - ☐ c. pride.
   - ☐ d. outrage.

9. Calvin McDowell, as seen in paragraph 4 of the selection, can be described as
   - ☐ a. meek and law-abiding.
   - ☐ b. a bully.
   - ☐ c. willing to stand up for himself.
   - ☐ d. a firm believer in nonviolence.

10. The point of view used in this selection is
    - ☐ a. third person limited.
    - ☐ b. third person omniscient.
    - ☐ c. second person.
    - ☐ d. first person.

Comprehension Skills

1. recalling specific facts
2. retaining concepts
3. organizing facts
4. understanding the main idea
5. drawing a conclusion
6. making a judgment
7. making an inference
8. recognizing tone
9. understanding characters
10. appreciating literary forms

VOCABULARY, PART TWO—

Write the word that makes the most sense in each sentence.

apathy	imperiling
proscriptions	harboring
provocation	

1. Wells-Barnett believed that as long as there was _____ and unconcern in the white community, lynchings of blacks would continue.

2. The _____ on lynchings which the law had put into place could be ignored at will in the South.

3. Blacks could be lynched for minor crimes and with little _____.

4. Those who were _____ racial hatred in their hearts showed their feelings by going along with lynchings.

5. People who spoke out against lynchings might be _____ their own lives.

scoffed	vigilance
obtains	inclination
conviction	

6. Wells-Barnett had a strong _____ that the only way things could be changed was to make more people aware of what was going on.

7. She said that the "indifference which so largely _____ regarding mob rule" should not, in fact, be customary at all.

8. She knew that the _____ to do evil was almost second nature in some people.

9. These people generally _____ at laws and refused to take them seriously.

114

10. To prevent lynchings, _____ was needed on the part of law-enforcement officers.

Comprehension Score [   ]

Vocabulary Score [   ]

WRITING —

Assume you are the wife, mother, or father of one of the men who were killed. Write a letter to the editor of a local white newspaper explaining your feelings about what happened. Use details from the selection to give substance to your letter.

STUDY SKILLS —

Read the following passage and answer the questions that follow it.

Taking Essay Examinations

Following certain rules and using certain techniques when taking examinations can result in higher grades. Procedures that organize and improve your performance permit you to use your knowledge of the subject to best advantage.

The essay or composition type is another kind of examination. This requires the student to compose responses to several questions. Many students dislike this type, preferring objective-type examinations. Yet knowing how to handle the written examination is important for successful test taking. Here are some rules to follow:

1. Outline Answers. Outline the answers to all questions before doing any writing. Restrict your outline to main headings only. Include a subhead only if you feel you may forget the information otherwise.

2. Balance Outlines. Look over all of your outlines. Some will be complete; others will be weak. Transfer some of the headings from the strong answers to the weak ones. This will give you confidence in answering. The questions are all on the same subject so a little deliberation will indicate how you can transfer headings and make them applicable to other questions.

3. Apportion Time. Divide your time proportionately. Base your time allotments on the credit value of the questions—spend more time on those that are worth more. If all of the questions are of equal value, devote equal time to each answer. This permits you to make your answers of generally similar length, concealing any weaknesses in your answers. A too-short answer signals the instructor that your knowledge on a certain question is lacking. Avoid giving such signals.

4. Write Legibly. Even if your answers are shorter as a result, take the time to make your handwriting clear and legible.

1. Knowing how to handle the _____ examination is important for successful test taking.

2. Headings in an answer outline can be _____ from the strong answers to the weak ones.

3. Spend more _____ on answers that are worth more—an explanation of what the lynching taught blacks, for example, rather than a simple recounting of what happened.

4. Lack of knowledge about a subject is often indicated by an answer that is too _____ .

5. Good handwriting that is clear and _____ is important in an essay examination.

Indictment of South Africa

Nelson Mandela

AUTHOR NOTES—
Nelson Mandela was born in 1918 at Umtata, on the Eastern Cape of South Africa. From his youngest days as a lawyer he was a political activist and a prominent figure in the black nationalist struggle against white South Africa's policy of apartheid.

After several imprisonments and skirmishes with South African authorities, Mandela was sentenced to life imprisonment in 1964 on charges of sabotage, treason, and conspiracy to overthrow the government by violence. Despite his isolation in prison, Mandela remained a symbol for the aspirations of South Africa's nonwhite majority. Finally, after pressure was applied by governments and antiapartheid groups around the world, Mandela was released from prison in 1990.

In 1990 Mandela's African National Congress and the white ruling party of South Africa agreed in principle to a new constitution under which all South Africans would have the right to vote. Mandela was elected president of South Africa in April, 1994.

VOCABULARY, PART ONE—
All of these terms are in the story you are about to read. Study each term and its meaning. Then answer the questions below.

As you read the story, notice how each vocabulary term is used. You will have more questions about the terms later.

striving, attempting; struggling for

disrepute, bad reputation

frequent, visit often

surveillance, a close watch

collective, gathered together; compiled

colleagues, fellow workers

sustained, supported; held up by

inculcation, constant teachings; brainwashings

subservience, submissiveness

abolished, done away with; eliminated

1. Which word names the characteristic of a wife who always gives in to everything her husband wants her to do? _____

2. Which word tells what the Emancipation Proclamation did to slavery?

    _____

3. Which word could name people who are employed with you on a job?

    _____

4. Which word could tell what you are doing if you are constantly working to improve your life? _____

5. Which word could name the job of detectives following a suspect around to check on his actions? _____

A READING PURPOSE—

In this selection, Mandela tells of the difficult life of blacks in South Africa and explains his feelings about the choices he has made. Read to discover what has motivated him.

1   Government violence can do only one thing and that is to breed counter-violence. We have warned repeatedly that the Government, by resorting continually to violence, will breed, in this country, counter-violence among the people till ultimately, if there is no dawning of sanity on the part of the Government, the dispute between the Government and my people will finish up by being settled in violence and by force. Already there are indications in this country that people, my people, Africans, are turning to deliberate acts of violence and of force against the Government, in order to persuade the Government in the only language which this Government shows, by its own behavior, that it understands.

2   Elsewhere in the world, a court would say to me "You should have made representations to the Government." This court, I am confident, will not say so. Representations have been made, by people who have gone before me, time and time again.

3   Nor will the court, I believe, say that, under the circumstances, my people are condemned forever to say nothing and to do nothing. If the court says that, or believes it, I think it is mistaken and deceiving itself. Men are not capable of doing nothing, of saying nothing, of not reacting to injustice, of not protesting against oppression, of not striving for the good society and the good life in the ways they see it. Nor will they do so in this country.

4   Perhaps the court will say that despite our human rights to protest, to object, to make ourselves heard, we should stay within the letter of the law. I would say, sir, that it is the Government, its administration of the law, which brings the law into such contempt and disrepute that one is no longer concerned in this country to stay within the letter of the law. I will illustrate this from my own experience. The Government has used the process of law to handicap me, in my personal life, in my career and in my political work in a way which is calculated, in my opinion, to bring a contempt for the law.

5   I found myself trailed by officers of the security branch of the police force wherever I went. In short, I found myself treated as a criminal, an unconvicted criminal. I was not allowed to pick my company, to frequent the company of men, to participate in their political activities, to join their organizations. I was not free from constant police surveillance any more than a convict in one of our jails is free from surveillance. I was made, by the law, a criminal, not because of what I had done, but of what I stood for, because of what I thought, because of my conscience. Can it be any wonder to anybody that such conditions make a man an outlaw of society? Can it be wondered that such a man, having been

outlawed by the Government, should be prepared to lead the life of an outlaw, as I have led for some months, according to the evidence before this court?

On trial and about to be sentenced to prison, Nelson Mandela warns of violence to come and a vow to take up the struggle upon being freed.

6 It has not been easy for me during the past period to separate myself from my wife and children, to say goodby to the good old days when, at the end of a strenuous day at an office, I could look forward to joining my family at the dinner table, and instead to take up the life of a man hunted continuously by the police, living separated from those who are closest to me, in my own country, facing continually the hazards of detection and of arrest. This has been a life infinitely more difficult than serving a prison sentence. No man in his right senses would voluntarily choose such a life in preference to one of normal family social life which exists in every civilized community.

7 But there comes a time, as it came in my life, when a man is denied the right to live a normal life, when he can live only the life of an outlaw because the Government has so decreed to use the law to impose a state of outlawry upon him. I was driven to this situation, and I do not regret having taken the decisions that I did take. Other people will be driven in the same way in this country, by this same very force of police persecution and of administrative action by the Government, to follow my course; of that I am certain.

8 I must place on record my belief that I have been only one in a large army of people, to all of whom the credit for any success of achievement is due. Advance and progress is the result not of my work, alone, but of the collective work of my colleagues and me, both here and abroad.

9 I do not believe, your worship, that this court, in inflicting penalties, will deter men from the course that they believe is right. History shows that penalties do not deter men when their conscience is aroused, nor will they deter my people or the colleagues with whom I have worked before.

10 I am prepared to pay the penalty even though I know how bitter and desperate is the situation of an African in the prisons of this country. I have been in these prisons and I know how gross is the discrimination, even behind the prison walls, against Africans, how much worse is the condition of the treatment meted out to African prisoners than that accorded to whites. More powerful than my fear of the dreadful conditions to which I might be subjected in prison is my hatred for the dreadful conditions to which my people are subjected outside prison throughout this country.

11 I hate the practice of race discrimination, and in doing so, in my hatred, I am sustained by the fact that the overwhelming majority of mankind hates it equally. I hate the systematic inculcation of children with color prejudice and I am sustained in that hatred by the fact that the overwhelming majority of mankind, here and abroad, is with me in that. I hate the racial arrogance which decrees that the good things of life shall be retained as the exclusive right of a minority of the population, and which reduces the majority of the population to subservience and inferiority, and maintains them as voteless chattels to work where they are told and behave as they are told by the ruling minority.

12 Nothing that this court can do to me will change in any way that hatred in me, which can only be removed by the removal of the injustice and the inhumanity which I have sought to remove from the political, social and economic life of this country.

13 Whatever sentence your worship sees fit to impose upon me for the crime for which I have been convicted before this court, may it rest assured that when my sentence has been completed I will still be moved, as men are always moved, by their consciences; I will still be moved to dislike of the race discrimination against my people when I come out from serving my sentence, to take up again, as best as I can, the struggle for the removal of those injustices until they are finally abolished once and for all.

Starting Time	
Reading Time	
Finishing Time	
■ Reading Rate	

COMPREHENSION —

Read the following questions and statements. For each one, put an X in the box before the option that contains the most complete or accurate answer.

1. Nelson Mandela says that, before his arrest, he was followed by
   - ☐ a. newspaper reporters.
   - ☐ b. autograph seekers.
   - ☐ c. security branch police officers.
   - ☐ d. judicial branch court officers.

2. Mandela warns that government violence will breed
   - ☐ a. counter-violence.
   - ☐ b. apathy.
   - ☐ c. debate.
   - ☐ d. neglect.

3. The facts in the selection are organized in
   - ☐ a. a cause-and-effect pattern.
   - ☐ b. ascending order.
   - ☐ c. chronological order.
   - ☐ d. spatial order.

4. The main idea that Mandela is offering is that
   - ☐ a. he wishes now he could go back to do things differently.
   - ☐ b. he believes in his cause but does not think it important enough to go to jail for.
   - ☐ c. nothing the government can do to him will change his determination to remove injustice.
   - ☐ d. the struggle for equality will go on without him, and putting him in prison is a futile measure.

5. We can conclude from the passage, and especially from Mandela's closing remarks, that he
   - ☐ a. is afraid of being imprisoned.
   - ☐ b. expects to be imprisoned.
   - ☐ c. expects to be let off with a warning.
   - ☐ d. is planning an appeal.

6. Based on Mandela's account, we can make the judgment that the South African government treated Mandela
   - ☐ a. fairly.
   - ☐ b. no differently than it treats any political dissident.
   - ☐ c. as an enemy to be harassed and persecuted.
   - ☐ d. with the respect of an old adversary.

7. It would be safe to infer that Mandela
   - ☐ a. had worked actively and visibly for justice in South Africa.
   - ☐ b. was mistakenly arrested.
   - ☐ c. promoted violence and had employed violent methods in the past.
   - ☐ d. does not expect to get out of prison alive.

8. The tone of the last half of the selection is
   - ☐ a. resigned.
   - ☐ b. hyperbolic.
   - ☐ c. disbelieving.
   - ☐ d. defiant.

9. To have endured the persecution to which he was subjected, Nelson Mandela must have been
   - ☐ a. strong and resourceful.
   - ☐ b. passive and forgiving.
   - ☐ c. emotional and hypersensitive.
   - ☐ d. intelligent but biased.

10. The address takes the form of
    - ☐ a. a plea.
    - ☐ b. an attack.
    - ☐ c. a letter.
    - ☐ d. a defense.

Comprehension Skills
1. recalling specific facts
2. retaining concepts
3. organizing facts
4. understanding the main idea
5. drawing a conclusion
6. making a judgment
7. making an inference
8. recognizing tone
9. understanding characters
10. appreciating literary forms

VOCABULARY, PART TWO —

Write the term that makes the most sense in each sentence.

striving   **frequent**
collective   **colleagues**
subservience

1. Mandela could not stand lowering himself to whites and showing _____ to them.

2. He had many _____ who pro-
   vided him company and supported his beliefs.

3. These people would _____ the
   same bars and restaurants and thus knew each
   other well.

4. All of them were _____ in any
   way possible to make conditions better in South
   Africa.

5. Their _____ work, taken as a
   whole, ought to have improved things some.

sustained   abolished
inculcation   disrepute
surveillance

6. Through propaganda and other forms of
   _____, blacks were taught to
   give in to whites in all things.

7. Anyone thought to be plotting against the government was put under close
   _____ and generally spied
   upon.

8. Protesters were _____ by their
   belief that they could make things better.

9. They knew that the government's unfairness
   brought all law into contempt and
   _____.

10. All their efforts were with the hope that apartheid
    would be _____.

Comprehension Score [   ]

Vocabulary Score [   ]

W R I T I N G —

Imagine that you are one of the judges Mandela is plead-
ing his case to and that you have decided he is innocent.
Write a few paragraphs explaining your decision. Use information from the selection to back up what you say.

S T U D Y   S K I L L S —

Read the following passage and answer the questions
that follow it.

How to Take Notes

It is an upsetting experience to attend a lecture and discover that you cannot possibly write fast enough to keep
up with the speaker. Actually the experience should not
be terrifying or frustrating, because a verbatim copy of
the lecturer's words is neither useful nor necessary.

Notetaking means simply that: taking notes on what
the speaker is saying—not making a transcript. To be
able to make notes on what is being said, it is important
to be listening—not hearing and copying, but listening,
and understanding the presentation.

A common student fault is that of writing instead of listening. If you do not understand the lecture in the classroom, you'll never piece it together meaningfully from your
notes. The first task of the notetaker, then, is to listen.

The value of notes taken in the classroom lies in their
association or recall power. Learn the topic of the lecture
and make a note of it. As the speaker progresses, listen
to what is being said on the topic and, while listening,
jot on paper the gist of the words, enough to trigger
later recall of the ideas.

The way notes are arranged should indicate the organization of the lecture. You should begin with a title for
the lecture; this goes at the top of the page. When the
speaker changes topics, start a new page.

Record the notes in an outline style. Main points are
listed, in order, at the margin, followed by a sentence or
two about them. Secondary ideas on the same point
should be indented and followed by a sentence of explanation. Further indentions indicate more subordinate ideas.
When you are reviewing the notes, a glance down the left-
hand margin will reveal all the main points of the lecture.

1. It is impossible to write down all the
   _____ of the speaker.

2. Your notes should trigger later
   _____ of ideas.

3. Arrangement of your notes should indicate the
   _____ of the lecture.

4. Main points are listed in order at the
   _____.

5. Notes about Nelson Mandela's speech, for example,
   might begin by noting that he is on _____.

120

BIBLIOGRAPHY

Angelou, Maya. *The Heart of a Woman*. New York: Random House, 1981.

———. *I Know Why the Caged Bird Sings*. New York: Random House, 1969.

Archer, Chalmers, Jr. *Growing Up Black in Rural Mississippi*. New York: Walker and Company, 1992.

Baldwin, James. *Go Tell It On the Mountain*. New York: The Dial Press, 1953.

Bambara, Toni Cade. "The Pill: Genocide or Liberation." In *Onyx*. New York: Onyx Publications, 1969.

Baraka, Amiri [LeRoi Jones]. *The Autobiography of LeRoi Jones*. New York: Freundlich Books, 1984.

Blay, J. Benibengor. "Funeral of a Whale." In *An African Treasury*. Edited by Langston Hughes. New York: Crown Publishers, 1960.

Bouwsma, Angela. "Showing His True Colors." In *Newsweek*, February 24, 1997.

Brown, H. Rap. *Die Nigger Die!* New York: The Dial Press, 1969.

Brown, Sterling. "Children of the Mississippi." In *The Collected Poems of Sterling A. Brown*. Edited by Michael S. Harper. New York: HarperCollins, 1980.

Carmichael, Stokley, and Charles V. Hamilton. *Black Power*. New York: Random House, 1967.

Clarke, John Henrik. "The Boy Who Painted Christ Black." In *American Negro Short Stories*. Edited by John Henrik Clarke. New York: Hill and Wang, 1966.

Cosby, Bill. *Fatherhood*. New York: Doubleday & Company, 1986.

———. "How to Win at Basketball: Cheat." In *Look*, January 27, 1970.

Cose, Ellis. *The Rage of a Privileged Class*. New York: HarperCollins, 1993.

Cullen, Countee. "Thoughts in a Zoo." In *My Soul's High Song*. Edited by Gerald Early. New York: Doubleday, 1991.

Danticat, Edwidge. "New York Day Women." In *Krik? Krak!* New York: Soho Press, 1995.

Douglass, Frederick. *My Bondage and My Freedom*, 1855.

———. *Narrative of the Life of Frederick Douglass, An American Slave*, 1845.

———. "What to the Slave Is the 4th of July?" In "Independence Day Address," 1852.

Dove-Danquah, Mabel. "Anticipation." In *An African Treasury*. Edited by Langston Hughes. New York: Crown Publishers, 1960.

Equiano, Olaudah. *Equiano's Travels: The Interesting Narrative of the Life of Olaudah Equiano, or Gustavus Vassa, the African*, 1789.

Farmer, James. *Lay Bare the Heart*. New York: Arbor House, 1985.

Gates, Henry Louis, Jr. *Colored People*. New York: Alfred A. Knopf, 1994.

Gregory, Dick, and Robert Lipsyte. *nigger*. New York: E. P. Dutton & Co., 1964.

Hansberry, Lorraine. *A Raisin in the Sun*. New York: Random House, 1958.

Hughes, Langston. "'Tain't So." In *The Book of Negro Humor*. Edited by Langston Hughes. New York: Dodd, Mead & Company, 1966.

Hurston, Zora Neale. *Dust Tracks on a Road*. Urbana, Illinois: University of Illinois Press, 1942.

Jackson, Reggie, with Mike Lupica. *Reggie*. New York: Villard Books, 1984.

Johnson, Charles. *Middle Passage*. New York: Penguin, 1990.

Jones, John H. "The Harlem Rat." In *Harlem U.S.A.* New York: Penguin, 1990.

Kincaid, Jamaica. *The Autobiography of My Mother*. New York: Farrar, Straus & Giroux, 1996.

King, Martin Luther, Jr. "A View from the Mountaintop." Martin Luther King, Jr. Estate, 1968.

Laye, Camara. *The Dark Child*. New York: Farrar, Straus & Giroux, 1954.

Mandela, Winnie. *Part of My Soul Went With Him*. New York: W. W. Norton & Company, 1985.

McMillan, Terry. *Disappearing Acts*. New York: Viking Penguin, 1989.

Morrison, Toni. *Jazz*. New York: Alfred A. Knopf, 1992.

———. *Sula*. New York: Alfred A. Knopf, 1973.

Naylor, Gloria. "Mattie Michael." In *The Women of Brewster Place*. New York: Viking Penguin, 1980, 1982.

Oates, Stephen B. *Let the Trumpet Sound: The Life of Martin Luther King, Jr.* New York: Harper & Row, 1982.

Page, Clarence. *Showing My Color: Impolite Essays on Race and Identity*. New York: HarperCollins, 1996.

Powell, Colin L. *My American Journey*. New York: Random House, 1995.

Reed, Ishmael. "Distant Cousins." In *Airing Dirty Laundry*. Reading, Massachusetts: Addison-Wesly, 1993.

Taulbert, Clifton L. *The Last Train North*. Tulsa: Council Oak Books, 1992.

Terry, Wallace. *Bloods: An Oral History of the Vietnam War by Black Veterans*. New York: Random House, 1984.

Walcott, Derek. "The Glory Trumpeter." In *Collected Poems, 1948–1984*. Farrar, Straus & Giroux, 1986

Walker, Alice. "Choice: A Tribute to Dr. Martin Luther King, Jr." In *In Search of Our Mother's Gardens: Womanist Prose*. New York: Harcourt Brace Jovanovich, 1983.

———. *The Color Purple*. New York: Harcourt Brace Jovanovich, 1982.

Walker, Margaret. *Jubilee*. Boston: Houghton Mifflin Company, 1966.

Washington, Booker T. *Up from Slavery: An Autobiography*, 1900.

Wideman, John Edgar. *Brothers and Keepers*. New York: Henry Holt and Company, 1984.

Wilkins, Roger. *A Man's Life: An Autobiography*. Simon & Schuster, Inc., 1982.

Wright, Richard. *Black Boy*. New York: Harper & Brothers, 1945.

Words-per-Minute Table

Selection # words	1	2	3	4	5	6	7	8	9	10	11	12	13	14	15	16	17	18	19	20
# words	1869	1540	1481	2010	312	1403	1599	1640	1768	1301	1442	1038	1047	301	1276	1645	1778	1067	1638	1213
1:20	1402	1155	1111	1508	234	1052	1199	1230	1326	976	1082	779	785	226	957	1234	1334	800	1229	910
1:40	1121	924	889	1206	187	842	959	984	1061	781	865	623	628	181	766	987	1067	640	983	728
2:00	935	770	741	1005	156	702	800	820	884	651	721	519	524	151	638	823	889	534	819	607
2:20	801	660	635	861	134	601	685	703	758	558	618	445	449	129	547	705	762	457	702	520
2:40	701	578	555	754	117	526	600	615	663	488	541	389	393	113	479	617	667	400	614	455
3:00	623	513	494	670	104	468	533	547	589	434	481	346	349	100	425	548	593	356	546	404
3:20	561	462	444	603	94	421	480	492	530	390	433	311	314	90	383	494	533	320	491	364
3:40	510	420	404	548	85	383	436	447	482	355	393	283	286	82	348	449	485	291	447	331
4:00	467	385	370	503	78	351	400	410	442	325	361	260	262	75	319	411	445	267	410	303
4:20	431	355	342	464	72	324	369	378	408	300	333	240	242	69	294	380	410	246	378	280
4:40	401	330	317	431	67	301	343	351	379	279	309	222	224	65	273	353	381	229	351	260
5:00	374	308	296	402	62	281	320	328	354	260	288	208	209	60	255	329	356	213	328	243
5:20	350	289	278	377	59	263	300	308	332	244	270	195	196	56	239	308	333	200	307	227
5:40	330	272	261	355	55	248	282	289	312	230	254	183	185	53	225	290	314	188	289	214
6:00	312	257	247	335	52	234	267	273	295	217	240	173	175	50	213	274	296	178	273	202
6:20	295	243	234	317	49	222	252	259	279	205	228	164	165	48	201	260	281	168	259	192
6:40	280	231	222	302	47	210	240	246	265	195	216	156	157	45	191	247	267	160	246	182
7:00	267	220	212	287	45	200	228	234	253	186	206	148	150	43	182	235	254	152	234	173
7:20	255	210	202	274	43	191	218	224	241	177	197	142	143	41	174	224	242	146	223	165
7:40	244	201	193	262	41	183	209	214	231	170	188	135	137	39	166	215	232	139	214	158
8:00	234	193	185	251	39	175	200	205	221	163	180	130	131	38	160	206	222	133	205	152
8:20	224	185	178	241	37	168	192	197	212	156	173	125	126	36	153	197	213	128	197	146
8:40	216	178	171	232	36	162	185	189	204	150	166	120	121	35	147	190	205	123	189	140
9:00	208	171	165	223	35	156	178	182	196	145	160	115	116	33	142	183	198	119	182	135
9:20	200	165	159	215	33	150	171	176	189	139	155	111	112	32	137	176	191	114	176	130
9:40	193	159	153	208	32	145	165	170	183	135	149	107	108	31	132	170	184	110	169	125
10:00	187	154	148	201	31	140	160	164	177	130	144	104	105	30	128	165	178	107	164	121
10:20	181	149	143	195	30	136	155	159	171	126	140	100	101	29	123	159	172	103	159	117
10:40	175	144	139	188	29	132	150	154	166	122	135	97	98	28	120	154	167	100	154	114
11:00	170	140	135	183	28	128	145	149	161	118	131	94	95	27	116	150	162	97	149	110
11:20	165	136	131	177	28	124	141	145	156	115	127	92	92	27	113	145	157	94	145	107
11:40	160	132	127	172	27	120	137	141	152	112	124	89	90	26	109	141	152	91	140	104
12:00	156	128	123	168	26	117	133	137	147	108	120	87	87	25	106	137	148	89	137	101
12:20	152	125	120	163	25	114	130	133	143	105	117	84	85	24	103	133	144	87	133	98
12:40	148	122	117	159	25	111	126	129	140	103	114	82	83	24	101	130	140	84	129	96
13:00	144	118	114	155	24	108	123	126	136	100	111	80	81	23	98	127	137	82	126	93
13:20	140	116	111	151	23	105	120	123	133	98	108	78	79	23	96	123	133	80	123	91
13:40	137	113	108	147	23	103	117	120	129	95	106	76	77	22	93	120	130	78	120	89
14:00	134	110	106	144	22	100	114	117	126	93	103	74	75	22	91	118	127	76	117	87
14:20	130	107	103	140	22	98	112	114	123	91	101	72	73	21	89	115	124	74	114	85
14:40	127	105	101	137	21	96	109	112	121	89	98	71	71	21	87	112	121	73	112	83
15:00	125	103	99	134	21	94	107	109	118	87	96	69	70	20	85	110	119	71	109	81

Minutes and Seconds Elapsed

Progress Graph

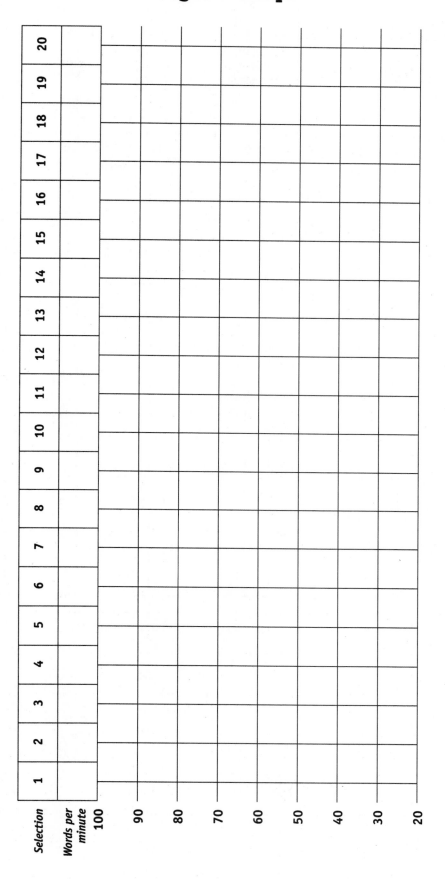

Comprehension Skills Profile

The graph below is designed to help you see your areas of comprehension weakness. Because all the comprehension questions in this text are coded, it is possible for you to determine which kinds of questions give you the most trouble.

On the graph below, keep a record of the questions you have answered incorrectly. Following each selection, darken a square on the graph next to the number of the question missed. The columns are labeled with the selection numbers.

By looking at the chart and noting the number of shaded squares, you should be able to tell which areas of comprehension you are weak in. A large number of shaded squares across from a particular skill signifies an area of reading comprehension weakness. When you discover a particular weakness, give greater attention and time to answering questions of that type.

Further, you might wish to check with your instructor for recommendations of appropriate practice materials.

Selection

Categories of Comprehension Skills	1	2	3	4	5	6	7	8	9	10	11
1. recalling specific facts											
2. retaining concepts											
3. organizing facts											
4. understanding the main idea											
5. drawing a conclusion											
6. making a judgment											
7. making an inference											
8. recognizing tone											
9. understanding characters											
10. appreciating literary forms											